# Journey to the Crown
## an alternative path to wellness

# Glenda Hodge

Published in 2016 by FeedARead.com Publishing

Copyright © Glenda Hodge www.holisticreflexology.com.au

First Edition

A CIP catalogue record for this title is available from the British Library.

# Acknowledgements

Thank you to my friends, colleagues and clients who have encouraged and supported all my ventures and projects over the years, with a special thank you to my Capricorn friend who helps me to structure and clarify my Piscean energy, concepts and ideas. Your honest assessment of my work is truly appreciated and valued.

To all those who have subscribed to my website, liked my Facebook Page or purchased my books, I trust that you have found them stimulating, and given you something to think about.

To the countless generous people who write informative articles on a variety of subjects, and freely share them online, your efforts are appreciated. While you may never see the results of all you do, I am sure you know that your words benefit thousands of people throughout the world.

I would also like to acknowledge the Arts Council England for the funding support they give to FeedARead, making publishing a manuscript easy, efficient and affordable. May I encourage all potential authors to consider FeedARead as your first option when it comes to publishing your book.

# Contents

# About the Author

For many years I lived with tunnel vision, contained within a narrow band of interest, paying little attention to what was outside the boundaries. I was relatively happy, having no visions to pursue, or urgent confronting problems to deal with.

In the late nineties, my higher consciousness led me to expand my parameters, move out of my comfort zone and engage in life in new and challenging ways.

Reflexology was the first step into my new world. Going to college introduced me to a world I didn't know existed, a place that held concepts and ideas I had never considered, and challenges that would take me well outside my comfort zone.

For the next sixteen years, I worked on feet in my reflexology practice, creating three busy clinics.

Many of the clients who came to see me were looking for answers. I don't fix anyone or solve problems; that is up to the person themselves. But these clients did start me thinking along alternative lines, and brought me to many of my own conclusions about pain, sickness, life and the reasons we are here.

These experiences taught me a lot, mostly about myself.

In 2010 my direction changed again. I needed to communicate what I had learnt through working with feet in my reflexology practice.

As I began to identify many of the issues that show up in the feet, and the messages they were trying to convey, I wrote *Holistic Reflexology, the eight principles*. I discussed the eight factors I consider in my holistic approach to my work.

As I encouraged my clients to take an alternative approach to life, I found myself telling many of my own stories to support my theories. These conversations led to my next book, *Wisdom in Retrospect, glancing back with insight to discover wisdom hiding in the shadows*, written under the pen name of my grandmother Emma Gilbert. It discusses 64 lessons I had learnt in life, with the intention of encouraging the reader to think about their own.

*Journey to the Crown* discusses energy flow in the subtle body, and how everyday life can be disrupted when blockages occur. The reader is invited to consider each energy centre of the body and its associated lifestyle issues, and encouraged to listen to and act upon the messages that the body is trying to convey.

While you may have heard these ideas before, every so often, someone comes along, and explains them a little differently. And, in listening to the different words, you may hear what is being said for the very first time.

Albert Einstein is quoted as saying:
*Imagination is more important than knowledge.*
*For knowledge is limited, whereas imagination embraces the entire world, stimulating progress, giving birth to evolution.*

So, I invite you to step into your imagination, and come with me on this journey.
You may be surprised what you discover.

# Introduction

Many ancient traditions speak of an energy flow and life-force, and how it permeates all of creation. Some call it Chi or Qi. Others name it Ki, Parana or the Great Spirit.

*Journey to the Crown* discusses energy in the subtle body, and how blockages can disrupt everyday life.

This life-giving invisible energy follows many pathways throughout the subtle body. These pathways meet at points known as chakras which could be described as swirling vortexes or wheels of energy where the subtle meets the physical, and the world of the unseen connects with reality as we know it.

Wellness, optimum health and a positive lifestyle depend on an uninhibited flow of this energy, but the complex nature of the human condition can unintentionally block the energy, resulting in pain, sickness or unpleasant circumstances, which are simply messages about something in life that needs attention.

Albert Einstein's great equation $E=mc^2$ teaches that energy and matter are interchangeable under certain circumstances. Therefore, if you don't listen to a message when it presents in the form of energy, it might well change form, and deliver itself as matter, so as to have a greater impact.

In understanding the seven main chakras and the energy they contain, you may be able to identify which area of your life is out of balance and in disharmony, allowing you to deal with a particular situation before it changes form to gain greater attention.

*Journey to the Crown* is written in three parts.

Part One: Chakra Wisdom
  Discusses the seven chakras.
  Identifies associated lifestyle issues.
  Proposes ideas which might heal any blockages.
  Presents the basic challenges that confront each chakra.
  Offers a worksheet to help you find your purpose and reach your potential.

Part Two: The Purpose of Pain

Considers why people need to be sick, the benefits of illness, and reasons not to get well.

Isolates each chakra area of the body and discusses some of the associated health issues.

Looks at each chakra area of the foot and discusses any relevant foot problem.

Part Three: Energy Shifts in Everyday Life

We all have our own chakra stories as energies realign, clear or balance. Some would be easily recognised as we consciously joined in the experience. Others may have become clearer in retrospect. Either way, they were transformational moments.

In sharing my seven chakra stories, I hope to remind you of your own, and the moments when blocked energy freed, giving you a little more clarity, bringing with it a greater sense of harmony and balance.

Wellness is the natural state, and results from balance and harmony on all levels: physical, mental, emotional and spiritual.

Therefore, the body is continually giving messages about what needs to be dealt with. Working with chakra energy will help to make the messages clearer. If you pay attention and respond willingly, you can be moved along with pressure equivalent to the touch of a feather, but when you refuse to listen, the pressure will increase.

When you ignore the more subtle messages, you could find that the lessons are delivered in a much more unpleasant way.

*Journey to the Crown* is written to encourage the reader to notice, identify and deal with simple problems in their early stages, rather than have them transform into a serious lifestyle issue or disease.

# A Basic Overview

## Base Chakra

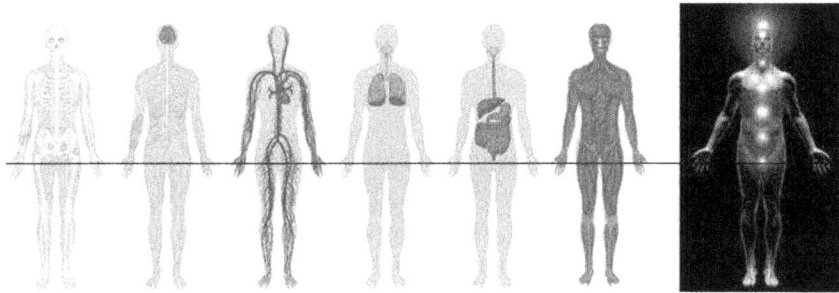

Lifestyle issues:
The ancestral line described as the family, groups, cultures, traditions, religions, beliefs and genes that you birthed yourself into. This chakra holds what your families and generations before them followed or belonged to. It provides security on an emotional level. This is the energy needed to ground you, and hold you secure in this physical reality.

Colour:
Red, the colour of earth, the foundations of our world, and the ground where your roots are planted.

Areas of the body: coccyx, pelvic area, reproductive organs, sigmoid colon, bladder.
Pain, symptoms and disease that present in these areas of the body are related in some way to family, tribe, group, religion or culture.

Health problems discussed:
Bladder cancer, coccyx injuries, constipation, diarrhoea, prostate cancer, sigmoid colon problems, urinary incontinence, urinary tract infections.

Foot problems discussed:
Blisters, cracks, callouses, plantar fasciitis, plantar warts, spurs, seed corns.

# Sacral Chakra

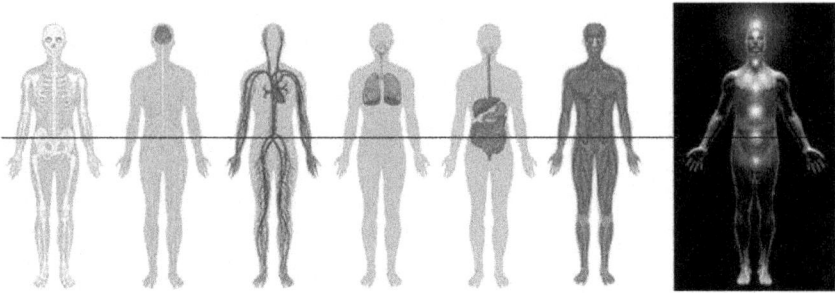

Lifestyle issues:
The sacral chakra energy will help you to discover yourself as an individual outside of the tribe, but you will only learn about yourself in relation to someone or something else. Therefore, this chakra focuses on relationships, to other people and material things.

Relationships with difficult people can fall into power games when you don't understand their purpose and how they work. The energy of this chakra is also concerned with your relationship to money, and the material security it can provide.

Colour:
Orange, the colour of autumn leaves. Each one falls independently of the other, leaving behind the security of belonging to the three. They may not be sure of what is ahead, as their season is bleak, but they know they are part of a cycle and summer will arrive without delay.

Areas of the body: sacrum, hips, gonads, lower back.
Pain, symptoms and disease that present in these areas of the body are related in some way to relationships, power games and material security including money and finances.

Health problems discussed:
Appendicitis, colon cancer, Crohn's disease, diverticulitis, endometriosis, infertility, irritable bowel syndrome, lower back pain, menopause, ovarian cancer, sciatica.

Foot problems discussed:
Fractured ankle, sprained ankle, plantar fasciitis, swollen ankles.

## Solar Plexus Chakra

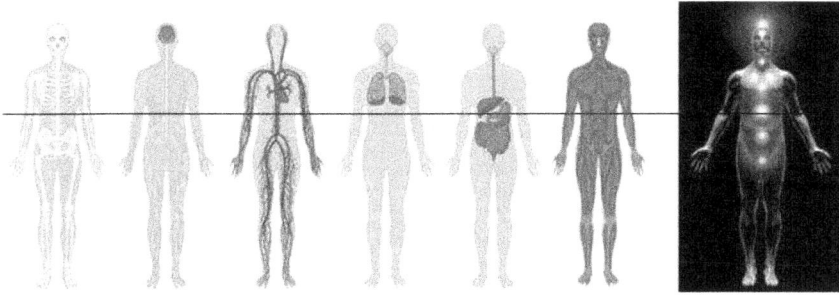

Lifestyle issues:
The solar plexus energy will establish and define you as an individual. It will help you to identify yourself, by setting your personal boundaries, and respecting those of others. It will allow you to honour yourself as you put yourself first.

And, while others may not understand and call you selfish, you know that this giant leap to self is an essential step on your journey to unlock the energy of your crown.

Colour:
Yellow, the colour that attracts attention; the colour of the sun from earth. This is the colour that reflects your individuality, draws attention to all you are, and allows you to shine in your own right. As yellow surrounds you, and becomes stronger, it lights up the darkness.

Areas of the body: lumbar spine, stomach, small intestine, pancreas, liver, gallbladder, lower thoracic spine, kidneys, adrenals.
Pain, symptoms and disease that present in these areas of the body are related in some way to the relationship with yourself, which includes your own boundaries and rules, and those of others.

Health problems discussed:
Celiac disease, gallstones, hiatus hernia, kidney failure, liver cancer, pancreatic cancer, reflux and heartburn, stomach cancer, stomach ulcers, type 1 diabetes, type 2 diabetes.

Foot problems discussed:
Fallen arches, high arches.

# Heart Chakra

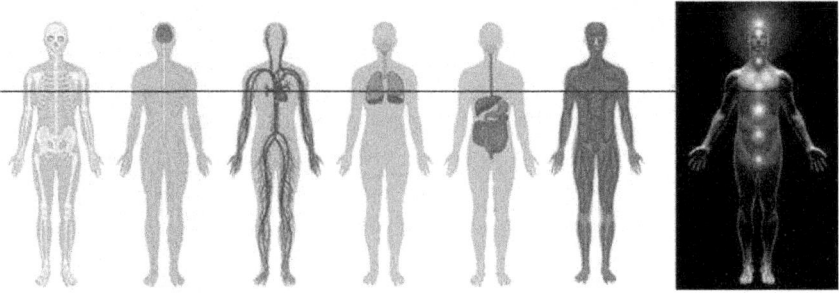

Lifestyle issues:
A vibrant heart chakra is the door to your higher self. You no longer need to understand everything, nor are you are controlled by emotions, other people or past beliefs. The heart merges logic, emotions and basic instincts to an indefinable knowing, a knowing that will lead you in safety, and urges you to follow.

You have reached a point in your life where you are able to recognise the wisdom of your inner guidance and the knowing of your heart.

Colour:
Green, the colour that enables the traveller to move forward in safety; the colour of unhindered passage. Green also signifies new growth, and buds that are ready to burst into blossom. Green holds a promise that something new is about to come forth. Go towards it with confidence.

Areas of the body: thoracic spine, heart, diaphragm line, lungs, breast.
Pain, symptoms and disease that present in these areas of the body are related in some way to flow and blockages, being on the right track and persistence.

Health problems discussed:
Aorta aneurysm, asthma, blood pressure, breast cancer, bronchitis, cardiovascular disease, cystic fibrosis, emphysema, fractured ribs, heart attack and hardening of the arteries, heart failure and cardiomyopathy, lung cancer.

Foot problems discussed:
Pain at ball of foot, bunion, gout, seed corns.

# Throat Chakra

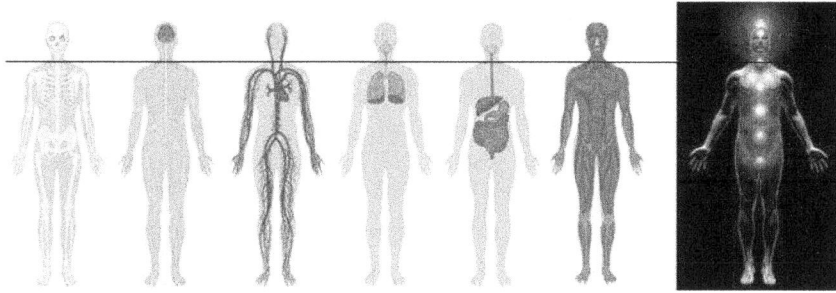

Lifestyle issues:
This chakra holds the energy for creating your own life circumstances through conscious choice, rather than existing within unexplained chaos. As you focus on your spoken or unspoken words, thoughts and beliefs, they create your reality. Underpinning their power is responsibility: an essential key to creating a life of choice.

If you are not responsible on some level of your consciousness for everything that shows up in your life, then you are powerless to make any changes. But, if you have created it, then you can change it. Personal responsibility is the power of creation.

Colour:
Blue, the colour of the heavens and the colour of the seas, combining what is visible and above, with what is hidden and below. In bringing them together, we create our reality.

Areas of the body: cervical spine referring to the shoulder, including axillary nodes, throat, thyroid, neck, tonsils.
Pain, symptoms and disease that present in these areas of the body are related in some way to taking responsibility, shouldering loads that aren't yours to carry, speaking up and flexibility.

Health problems discussed:
Dislocated shoulder, frozen shoulder, fused vertebrae, goitre, Grave's disease, Hashimoto's disease, jaw problems, lymphoma, mouth ulcer, rotator cuff tear, sore throat, stiff neck, tonsillitis.

Foot problems discussed:
Tinea, webs of toes.

# Third Eye Chakra

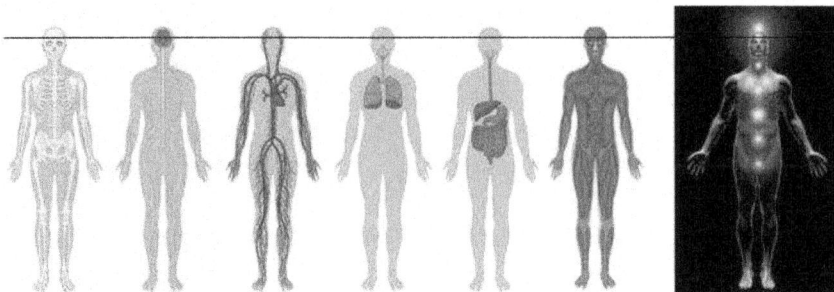

Lifestyle issues:
The energy of the third eye will take you past the physical, the logical and the explainable, as it invites you to move through the three dimensions of the physical world into the realms of the unknown.

This energy asks you to re-evaluate your beliefs, and reconsider life from a higher perspective. It invites you to open your mind and pursue possibility, be comfortable with the unexplained, and offer no judgment. It challenges you to look again at everything you have come to know, believe and value through the vision and clarity of a perspective greater than your logical mind can understand.

Colour:
Purple, the preference of royalty, the colour of amethyst, and an expression of wisdom. The promise awaits you. When you step aside from the masses, and consider life from a higher perspective, wisdom awaits you.

Areas of the body: nose, sinuses, eyes, ears, and pineal, pituitary and hypothalamus glands.
Pain, symptoms and disease that present in these areas of the body are related in some way to closing the mind, making something right or wrong, opening up to the paranormal and unexplained, or being overly logical and analytical.

Health problems discussed:
Sinusitis, hearing loss, dry eyes, macular degeneration, Meniere's disease, insomnia, frontal headache, tinnitus, vertigo.

Foot problems discussed:
Arthritis, paronychia.

# Crown Chakra

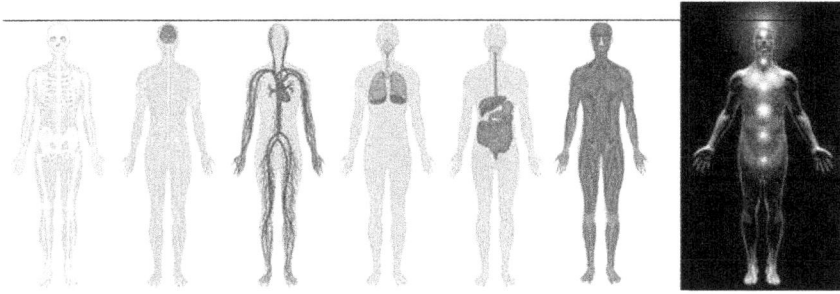

Lifestyle issues:
The crown chakra is the doorway to your innate spiritual nature. Its purpose is to dissolve the ego and unite with spirit. It seeks to break down the barriers of illusion, so you can understand the oneness of all creation.

The crown makes sense of the past, shows hope for the future, and brings understanding to the chaos. And, it leads you to understand that life is perfect, all is well, and everything has always been on your terms.

Colour:
White, the place where all the colours of the rainbow combine and become one. A perfect parallel to the world and all it contains.

Areas of the body: Brain, skull, hair.
Pain, symptoms and disease that present in these areas of the body are related in some way to trust and vulnerability, letting go of control and ego, connecting to spirit, self-mastery and transformation.

Health problems discussed:
Brain tumour, brain aneurysm, fractured skull, dementia, multiple sclerosis, cerebral palsy, Parkinson's disease, headaches, stroke, meningitis, spina bifida, head lice.

Foot problems discussed:
Curled toes, ingrown toenails.

# Part I

## Chakra Wisdom

This section discusses the seven chakras, and proposes how wellness, potential and lifestyle can be disrupted when energy flow becomes blocked. It invites the reader to isolate the areas of their life that don't flow freely, and consider what could be the underlying cause of the problem.

The journey to the crown begins with the tribe, where you redefine your place within it, or your need to move away. For those who distance themselves, many will look for another tribe or another person to belong to.

As you realise that security doesn't depend on another or material possessions, you begin to honour yourself, define your boundaries, and acknowledge your own needs as a priority.

Your heart fills with gratitude, for you understand that everything in your life is on your terms; nothing has ever happened without your consent on some level of your consciousness. You begin to trust and follow your intuition.

In taking responsibility for everything in your reality, you empower yourself.

In letting go of judgment, you open your mind to possibility.

And in reaching the crown, you connect with something far greater than your physical body, and you understand that everything is perfect, there are no mistakes and all is well.

You make this journey from the base to the crown over and over again throughout your lifetime – sometimes on a daily basis – and every so often, something unexpectedly appears, bringing forth a reaction you were not prepared for.

The journey to your higher self can be filled with challenges, but as you grow in awareness, your understanding of such challenges will change.

And so, each chakra discussed includes a worksheet to help you identify where any unexpected responses might have originated, why there may be disharmony in certain areas of your life, and will encourage you to continue along your pathway to find your purpose and reach your potential.

May you notice, identify and deal with simple problems in their early stages. May you act on what you have learnt and be brave enough to move beyond your comfort zone in finding resolution.
May you enjoy the adventure of your own journey.

# Base Chakra

The two most important days in your life are
The day you are born
and
The day you find out why
Mark Twain

The base chakra embraces the ancestral heritage that you were born into: the family, groups, cultures, traditions, religions, beliefs and genes. It holds what your families and generations before them followed or belonged to.

This is the place where your basic primal instincts hide or reside:
Survival skills that keep you safe in a changing world.
Secret behaviour patterns that control your life.
Deep and entrenched beliefs that can bring forth bias and rejection of others.
Reactions which are inconsistent with conscious choice and potential.

The energy of the base is needed to ground you, and hold you secure in this physical reality. It is primarily interested in survival, one of the strongest forces in nature. It will often compromise potential to achieve this end.

An un-evolved base chakra isn't particularly interested in a higher purpose as it can find a false sense of security in the physical and does not pursue the spiritual.

Your ancestors or 'the tribe', as it is often called, can be dictatorial. You need to honestly assess whether the beliefs of the tribe that you currently hold encourage and support your higher purpose and potential.

## Related issues

Your relationship to the group.
Your place in the family, tribe, society, tradition, religion or culture.
Family dynamics.
Childhood.
Emotional security.
Ability to integrate into the wider community.
A sense of not belonging or not feeling part of something.
Religious beliefs and cultural traditions.
Rules of the group that must be obeyed.
Hierarchy.
Family beliefs that you have inherited.
Basic survival instincts.
Behavioural patterns and habits.
Reactions rather than a choice-centred response.

## Healing the Base Chakra

### I chose my path before I came

This approach presupposes that a person incarnates more than once. Believing that everyone comes into this world through choice, bringing with them their purpose for being here helps to explain some of life's more difficult challenges. Not every person, religion, culture or tradition believes in past, simultaneous or other lifetimes. Therefore, this method of healing the base chakra may not resonate with everyone. But, then again, this may be an opportunity to re-evaluate such a belief.

In spirit we make a contract before we incarnate into this life experience. We agree to certain events before we come – some positive, others negative – which could well be described by a value system as good or bad, right or wrong. Then we place ourselves into the best possible position to achieve what we have chosen. We put ourselves directly into our unfolding story. We choose the family, the culture, the circumstances, the time frame and the experience all in advance.

Therefore life becomes just another chapter in a much bigger story that is not held in the conscious memory.

In healing the base chakra a person needs to consider the family, group, culture, traditions, religion and beliefs that they have placed themselves into.

Then, they need to acknowledge the positives of what they have learnt from them.

Too often people are overcome by emotions, focus on the negatives, and miss the reason as to why they chose their particular circumstances.

When someone is born into a life that is difficult, they could be:
Bringing balance to something they have done in other lifetimes.
Taking on a difficult and challenging role to teach and help others.
Taking on the role of evil or bad as there are experiences of forgiveness, comradeship, bravery and love to be had.


## Identifying core beliefs

Any beliefs, behaviour patterns, inappropriate reactions or unacceptable responses that do not serve your highest good need to be identified and either released or modified, so that they will not sabotage your potential.

To discover these beliefs and patterns, look at the area/s of your life that don't work as you would like them to, and ascertain what you believe about them.

While beliefs and patterns were originally taken up in childhood, they are reinforced in just about every area of life from then on, not necessarily in a direct way, but indirectly over and over again through culture, religion, family, traditions and governments. Not everyone embraces all of them. Some tribes focus on one in preference to another, and each generation has their own exclusive expression.

There would appear to be four common beliefs that were generally learnt in childhood. These serve as an umbrella for many others.

## I am powerless

To fit into the acceptable parameters that maintained the order or chaos of the family, some children learnt powerlessness: the ability to contain their inner core and suppress their truest self for the good of others. It was as though they lost their true sense of identity by not being able to express their deepest needs, desires and dreams. The family rules to maintain order more than likely squashed the child, rather than supported them until they could stand in their own power and strength. Self-empowerment was disbursed and weakened until it almost disappeared, and was feared.

The powerless adult will often not speak up for themselves and stay in the background, convinced that they cannot contribute or make a difference.

These people may have lived under such strict rules and commands that their spirit of enthusiasm and expression was squashed or damaged.

Until they can speak with their own voice of authority, power will never belong to them, and until they take control of their lives, others will control them.

There are many ways a child could have been disempowered. Identifying the cause may help the adult who still carries that particular belief.

Recall the sayings, commands, directions and demands that were continually repeated in the child's household, and if they were suppressive in any way. What were the negative things you remember being said over and over again?

While rules can be helpful to create and maintain harmony in a community, some rules can be oppressive and limiting. What were your childhood rules?

Some religious beliefs can encourage a feeling of powerlessness, in the sense that God is in control and people are dependent on mercy. Did anyone in your family every wonder why God let certain things happen, and why bad things happened to good people?

## I am not good enough

When a child's constant best efforts were negated and judged as not satisfactory, they might begin to believe that there was something wrong with them. They may also become competitive to prove their worth. If rewards, praise and accolades were connected to what they achieved, they could learn that doing something and achieving something was more important than being someone.

The adult who believes they are not good enough in their own right, and that their self-worth comes from what they do and produce, may become a workaholic to prove themselves. The need to prove that they are as good as others may develop an extremely competitive personality with the need to excel.

Adults who still carry this belief may need to be constantly recognised and approved of, and to be the centre of attention to make up for any lack of recognition in the past.

If a person believes that they are not good enough, they may also believe that they are undeserving, and so create patterns of self-sabotage, self-destruction or self-punishment.

There are many ways a child could have learnt that they were not good enough. Identifying the cause may help the adult who still carries that particular belief.

Siblings could have constantly been compared, with one not matching up to the other, or parental expectations not being met.

Ingratitude may have been instilled into a child, as the parent constantly reminded them of all that they had done for them or gone without in providing for their needs. This could result in the adult child spending their life, filled with guilt, trying to repay the parent.

In trying to please and win approval because you did not feel you were good enough as you were, you may have compromised yourself to become the good child. This could have progressed to the good wife, the good neighbour and other images you want to present, rather than your authentic self.

Sayings especially related to a comparison with someone or something could have had a profound effect on your self-worth and convince you that you would never amount to anything much.

This belief is subtly re-enforced even in children's songs, *He knows when you've been bad or good, so be good for goodness sake*. Santa Claus doesn't come to naughty children. If you aren't good enough, you won't get any Christmas presents.

## Love will bring me pain

A child could readily connect love with pain when someone they love leaves or dies, and they are overwhelmed with loss and sadness.

Being rejected, abandoned or betrayed by someone they loved and trusted would most probably have been painful in many ways.

Children can be quite subjective and when they don't get something they desperately want, they can feel hurt, sad or unloved.

The workload of busy parents could limit one-on-one time with a child and be open for misinterpretation. Financial needs could have demanded working long hours away from the family. Exhausted parents who needed time away from family pressures to rejuvenate could have been judged as selfish and unloving.

Sibling favouritism could be another reason for a child to connect love with pain, if they needed to compete to gain the love and attention of a parent.

The adult who connects love with pain may resist committing to relationships, resulting in being isolated, cut off, distant or having strong emotional boundaries to keep others out. They may also reject a relationship because the thought of unfilled hopes and dreams, together with the possibility of loss or disappointment, are too big a risk to take. The trust involved in loving can place a person in a vulnerable position which is difficult for someone who needs to be in control of the outcome.

Television, reading, hobbies, sport, or addictive habits may be a safer companion than a loving relationship, as these can be on an individual's own terms with no consideration for another.

Love requires a commitment. Commitment can be painful when it limits freedom and options.

There are many ways a child could have learnt to connect love with pain. Identifying the cause may help the adult who still carries that particular belief.

The most obvious way a child would have taken this belief upon themselves was with the death of someone they loved, or even a pet they loved.

Parents who fought and argued when they were supposed to love each other could challenge the child's idea of what love was supposed to be. When disagreement resulted in separation and divorce, the child could also be torn apart in some way.

Love and suffering are inseparable in the Christian tradition. God so loved the world that he gave his only son Jesus to die on the cross. *Spare the rod and spoil the child* was a common saying from the Bible. Therefore, if you love your child, you will discipline them, strongly, when required. Men and women who held strongly religious views about marriage believed it to be a lifelong commitment. There was to be no escape when love turned to pain except for death.

## The world isn't a safe place

A child might expect the home environment to be a safe haven but if domestic violence, child abuse, illness, drugs or alcohol share the family home, the child might end up living in a volatile situation where safety is an issue.

The over-protective parent can transfer their own fears on to the child without realising it.

Children need stability for security. Civil wars, refugees and terrorism are all part of an unsafe world.

The adult who holds the conviction that the world isn't safe or sustainable may have had this belief reinforced in many ways. Governments can emphasise how unsafe the world is by over-legislation. World news comes into the home every day bringing stories of death, murder, mishap, natural disasters, wars, terror attacks, endangered species or the deteriorating state of the planet.

The person who believes that the world is unsafe may surround themselves with possessions and other things they enjoy, so as to create a safe environment. This could be misinterpreted as materialism but in reality it may only be a safety net because they believe the world isn't safe. They may also become a hoarder as they believe that the world isn't sustainable and there isn't enough to go around.

As adults they may lack the spirit of adventure to avoid any mishaps and danger, or suffer with addictions to create an escape from a world that isn't safe.

There are many ways a child could have learnt that the world isn't a safe place or sustainable environment. Identifying the cause may help the adult who still carries that particular belief.

An unpredictable parent due to mental health issues, alcohol or drugs could have created an unsafe environment for other members of the family. Television advertisements aimed at domestic violence and driving under the influence of alcohol or drugs also confirm the dangers that are often close by.

If a parent or primary carer dies, then a child could fear the future without them close by to protect them, especially if the family is poor with few resources, or unable to provide basic necessities.

Parents' constant reminders about talking to strangers can be a safeguard, but also unsettling.

Overly supervised playtime because someone may get hurt can be a fear of the parent being passed down to the children. Schoolyard and cyberbullying can be disturbing and difficult to escape.

World news enters our homes daily, bringing with it graphic images of senseless killings of innocent people, the plights of those from war zones, the effects of cruel dictatorships, and the fragile environment with many species dying.

Violent animations and movies unsuitable for children are easily accessible.

In identifying if and how any of these beliefs still play a role in the life of the adult, you may recognise the changes that need to be made before the energy of this chakra becomes dense and blocked, creating a situation which will be more complex and harder to dissipate.


## In Summary

You have a life purpose that you chose before you came to the earth.
You chose all of the circumstances that you birthed yourself into.
On some level of your consciousness you have allowed, created or drawn to yourself your own reality.
Value what you have created and be open to its lessons.
Refuse to blame anyone for what is happening in your life.
You are not a victim.

Make changes to your inherited beliefs if they do not serve your highest purpose.

Recognise your behavioural patterns that keep you locked into survival mode.

Living in a community or society requires guidelines to maintain stability.

Re-evaluate the cost you pay to belong.

Ground your spiritual beliefs by putting them to work for you in a practical way.

Love the earth. Take care of it. Be environmentally aware.


## The Challenge

Do you still belong to the tribe? If so, where you stand in relation to it?

The cost of belonging: what you have done in the past, or what you continue to do, to survive there?

Does it still serves your highest potential, or demand compromise?

What is the appropriateness of the survival techniques it taught you?

## Worksheet

The purpose of the worksheet to help you identify where any unexpected responses might have originated, why there may be disharmony in certain areas of your life, and encourage you to continue along your pathway to find your purpose, and reach your potential.

It is often said that closure to something is found at the beginning. Revisiting any difficult experience from a spiritual perspective invites a person to remember that on some level of their consciousness they allowed, created or drew to themselves everything that happened. They are not victims of anyone or anything. They created or joined in scenarios to learn, teach or give. They are the one responsible for the experience.

However, many people do not revisit past experiences from such a perspective and find the meeting very difficult.

In looking at the base chakra and all the relative issues from the perspective that you created them yourself, I hope to encourage you to stand back, and focus on a much bigger picture which isn't always obvious.

### Choosing your basic group

If you do not believe in other lifetimes, for the purpose of this exercise, pretend for a moment that you chose this one, and placed yourself into your unfolding story.

- What might your particular family, tradition, culture or religion encompass or contain so as to be the perfect environment for you to grow, evolve and reach your potential in this lifetime?

- Can you identify how certain people in your family/group are helping you achieve this?

28

- You may have come to break down entrenched family patterns, and free up your past and future ancestral line. Can you recognise any family cycles and patterns which you are caught up in, and the ones you can help to dismantle?

**Lessons to learn**

Discovering your life purpose can be a slow on-going process which is not very clear at the beginning. Quite often you need to discover who you are not, before you can begin to know who you are. While you may not know what you want, you may be more aware of what you don't want.

Therefore, experiences described as negative could be the shortcut to your direction in life. As you begin to understand who or what you don't want to become, who or what you want to become appears clearer.

Even when the positives are hidden, they are still there, but it is easy to become overwhelmed by negative emotions, and lose the meaning and potential behind the difficult choices that some people make.

- What are the positive things that your particular family, tradition, culture or religion taught you about yourself, even if they were learnt through negative experiences?

**Hidden beliefs**

To discover the hidden beliefs that control your life, pick an area of your life that doesn't function as you would like it to. Write down what you believe about it, in as much detail as possible.

Nothing comes into your consciousness unless it is an issue that needs to be addressed. Often acknowledgement is a big part of moving forward.

• Your beliefs about      .....................

**Learnt behavioural patterns**

My grandmother taught me that children should be seen and not heard. I had to learn to speak up, and say what I thought. If I hadn't addressed that pattern, I would never have been able to write any of my books.

• What behavioural patterns did you learn in childhood?

• As an adult, are these patterns still active or appropriate, and how do they affect your life?

**Negative sayings**

*What will the neighbours think?* I learnt that it was important what the neighbours, and everybody else for that matter, thought. I now know that I don't need the approval of others. I only need to approve of myself.

- What negative sayings were often repeated in your family during your childhood?

- As an adult, can you recognise the implications of these sayings, and if they still have any effect on you?

**What you figured out**

I decided my best option was to do as I was told. As an adult, remnants of that stayed with me for a long time. Being told what to do was part of my life for many years. Over time, I seemed to address it in some areas, but didn't come close in others.

- What were some things you figured out for yourself as a child?

- As an adult, did you find that what you figured out for yourself as a child was still appropriate?

**Spontaneous reactions**

For many years my immediate reaction to something that didn't turn out as expected was to ask myself, *what did I do wrong?* I was always ready and willing to take the blame in some way.

- What were your most common spontaneous reactions as a child?

- As an adult, in a similar situation, how would your conscious choice differ from spontaneous reaction?

In identifying the reason you chose your family, and what they taught you, be it through negative or positive means, hopefully you can identify your strengths and talents, and begin to understand where these are guiding you to.

In identifying the hidden beliefs, behaviour patterns and negative sayings that you learnt in your survival days, you might now understand what is underneath any inappropriate responses, and whether what you figured out for yourself is still relevant.

Awareness is the beginning of change. Knowing what is hiding in your subconscious waiting to influence your responses or manipulate your actions is the first step to dismantling what is not serving the pathway to your higher consciousness. Acting on what you learn, even if it is only in a small way, is the next step on your journey to the crown.

Once you become disillusioned with the tribe, you begin to move away, but all too often you are not strong enough to stand alone, and immediately look for another group to join, or a relationship to enter. You can move from tribe to tribe and relationship to relationship for many years, looking to others for support, strength and security.

You are moving away from being the same as everyone else to having your own individual values, and sacrificing the security of the tribe, to find security in other ways and in other places.

# Sacral Chakra

*It is not the strongest of the species that survives,*
*nor the most intelligent that survives.*
*It is the one that is most adaptable to change.*
*Charles Darwin*

The sacral chakra energy will help you to discover yourself as an individual if you understand how it works. You will only learn about yourself in relation to someone or something else. This chakra focuses its energy on relationships: your relationship to another and your relationship to money, and the security these bring.

Many intense learning experiences break down into power games and struggles because you don't understand that you set them up in the first place to learn about yourself. When relationships are unpleasant you may not recognise yourself in the other person because you are focusing on the negative and what they are doing to you.

In contrast, if you were able to recognise a situation as a learning experience and focus on what you were learning about yourself, some of the more painful relationships would be understood in a totally different context.

You may think that a good relationship is your life's goal when in reality it is only a means to an end, discovering who you are. You may also think that money will guarantee financial security, when in fact it is your belief about money that is more important.

When you finally realise that your sense of belonging, your security and your rules come from within, you eventually learn to stop looking to others for answers. You realise that it is the relationship with yourself that is paramount. But, until you find yourself, you will search outside yourself for the answers to life.

## Related issues

One-on-one relationships.
Your ability to connect with others.
Sexuality.
Creative expression.
Children.
Gathering and depending on material possessions for security.
Money.
Power games.
Manipulation.
Aggressive competition.
Using people.

# Healing the Sacral Chakra

## Like attracts like

The principle of *like attracts like* is often dispelled and rejected because a person does not initially recognise themselves in the other. When we refuse to acknowledge our negatives, or fail to recognise our potential greatness, someone will come along to reflect these back to us.

Everyone in your life is a reflection of you in some way. What they reflect back to you is foremost your issue, not theirs.

The other person will share a common issue with you, but will more than likely express it differently to the way you do. If you focus on how the other person expresses this common issue you may never recognise yourself in them, and what they are trying to bring to your attention. You may not be able to see yourself in their reflection, because your focus is in the wrong place.

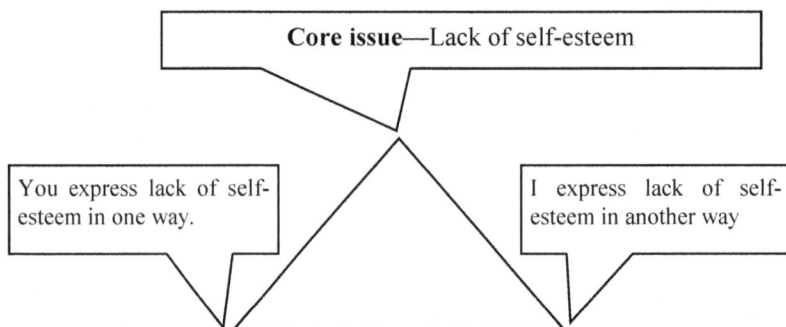

```
                    ┌────────────────────────────────────────┐
                    │   Core issue—Lack of self-esteem        │
                    └────────────────────────────────────────┘

  ┌─────────────────────────┐          ┌─────────────────────────┐
  │ You express lack of self-│          │ I express lack of self- │
  │ esteem in one way.       │          │ esteem in another way   │
  └─────────────────────────┘          └─────────────────────────┘
```

As long as I focus on how you express your lack of self-esteem, I may never identify what the common issue is that we share.

34

## Difficult people and power games

When someone is 'pressing your buttons' they are trying to get your attention, and help you identify something in your life that needs to be addressed. They are bringing up a particular issue for you because you are not able to begin the process yourself.

When it is time to let go of or acknowledge something, someone will come along and draw attention to it. It is easy to miss the opportunity because you can be so focused on what the other person is doing that you don't consider for a moment that the situation is actually about you.

Often the problem at hand isn't the real issue. The current problem is setting off something much deeper that is unresolved, and needs to be addressed.

**Power games only evolve when you interpret a given situation as someone doing something TO you, rather than someone doing something FOR you**

## Law of Attraction

You don't attract who and what you want to be, you attract who and what you are. By changing who you are, you change who and what you attract.

You are what you believe. Your reality is created from the blueprint of your beliefs. What you believe, you think about. What you think about with passion and emotion, you create.

It's a very simple formula. It works whether you understand it or not, consciously apply it or not, believe it or not.

For the open-minded person on a conscious journey through life, beliefs are easily changed, but there are many reasons why people hang on to outdated beliefs.

A person may believe that *drugs are an escape from a painful reality*. If or when that belief changes to *drugs are destroying my life*, the person changes, and the reality around them changes also.

A person doesn't just give up drugs. They also give up the environment they have lived in, the friends and connections they have made and the whole dynamic that their lifestyle had embraced.

If a person changes their religious beliefs and leaves the church community they could be ostracised from long-standing friendships.

If a person disputes strongly held family beliefs, disruptions to the family could cause splits and disharmony.

A person may find that their career choice isn't as fulfilling as they first believed, but the challenge of more study and finding another job could be overwhelming.

People can become so entrenched in their way of life, that they are not able to see there are other options available.

They may choose to stay with something they no longer believe in for many reasons: to maintain their social networks, because it has become a habit, or because it's easier than beginning again.

## Marrying the parent

We choose our parents for a specific reason. If we connect to or clone one of them, and don't especially learn from the other, it is quite possible that we will marry or partner a person with the attributes of the parent we didn't connect to or learn from. In retrospect it is often quite obvious which parent a person marries or partners.

When relationships continue to fail, it is possible that a person is not learning critical lessons necessary to their evolution. They continue to take the old stuck self forward time and time again.

Soul mates are not necessarily a best friend. They are those people who extend your boundaries so that you can learn about your own strength and potential.

## In summary

Everyone in your life is a reflection of you in some way.
Nobody does anything to you. They are doing something for you.
Nobody does anything to you without your permission on some level of your consciousness.
You learn about yourself in relationship to someone or something else.
Power games erupt when you don't understand the purpose of relationships.
Search for the positive in any situation to discover your inner strengths.
Let go of jealousy and competition, as we are all here for different reasons.
Learn to complement the other, rather than compete with them.
While the spiritual perspective respects the physical, emotional, and mental responses that a person may have experienced, it invites them to look at life from a higher plane.

## The Challenge

To see a difficult person as doing something for you rather than doing something to you.

To search until you recognise yourself in difficult people or those you don't like.

To look within for your security, not to other people and money.

# Worksheet

**Recognising yourself in another**

An example:

A certain person you know tells lies. It is an expression of low self-esteem.

You express low self-esteem in a different way. You express it by being extremely self-critical.

If you do not tell lies, then you may never recognise yourself in someone who does. When you understand that lies are only an expression of something else, you may be able to recognise your common ground, and the issue that you share.

Think of a person who upsets you; someone you would prefer to have nothing to do with, or be around.

• What do they do that upsets you so much?

Can you recognise that this action is an expression of something else; something that you both share?

• Identify and name the issue. This is the core issue you both share; the issue you have in common.

You express the same issue in a different way.

• Identify how you express the same issue.

By identifying the common issue you share with another, you will clearly see where you need to make changes in your own life.

If you do not recognise what is being reflected back to you about yourself, you could miss an opportunity for personal growth and development.

## Difficult people

Think of a difficult person in your life.

- What do they do or say that upsets you?

- How do they make you feel?

The feelings that are surfacing are setting off and bringing to the surface other unresolved issues.

- Can you recognise your own unresolved issues that the behaviour of this difficult person could be setting off?

Difficult people are not doing anything TO you; they are doing something FOR you.

Your higher consciousness knows that you are ready to deal with a particular issue and allows someone else to begin the process.

The sooner you recognise that the person is actually doing something for you, and begin to address the issue, the dynamic with that person will change.

Why?

Because you got the message they were trying to deliver. Their job is done.

**Beliefs and thoughts**

When beliefs are changed, thoughts follow. Beliefs can be changed in an instant. Thoughts may take a little longer for a person who hasn't learnt how to control their mind and thinking.

In identifying your beliefs, you may be able to see the effect they have had on your life.

Some of my beliefs:

Pain, disease and symptoms are trying to draw my attention to something in my life that needs to be addressed.

What I believe, I think about. What I think about with focus and emotion, I create.

Energy cannot be created nor destroyed. It merely changes form.

Chaos comes before order.

I am responsible for everything in my life.

My essence is far greater than the mind can comprehend.

- Your beliefs:

- Can you recognise how each of your beliefs has impacted upon a specific situation that has shown up in your life?

**Who did you marry or partner?**

There may have been essential lessons that you needed to learn in your childhood, and somehow you missed them. It's never too late to learn. If you missed them in your parents, it's more than likely you will marry or partner them.

- What qualities or habits of your parent/s do you recognise in your spouse/partner?

You will only learn about yourself in relation to someone or something else. Other people, especially difficult people, are working with you, on a level you may not understand, to bring your own issues to your attention.

Your higher self knows that it is time to address them, but quite often you will need some help in beginning the process. Recognising yourself in others, and more especially understanding the role of difficult people in your life, is a fast track to moving along your pathway, on your journey to the crown.

Recognising which parent you partner allows you to discover what you didn't learn in childhood, and embracing your own personal beliefs, provides the infrastructure to create a life of choice without tribal intervention, but that may somewhere in the future, a little further down your pathway.

You are moving away from being the same as everyone else to having your own individual values, and sacrificing the security of the tribe to find security in other ways and in other places. As you learn about your strengths and abilities, you grow in self-confidence and self-worth. As you value and define yourself, you honour who you are, your boundaries and the boundaries of others.

You have moved from finding security in the tribe, to finding security in another or something else. You are now ready to allow the solar plexus energy to flow freely and honour yourself and your own rules by putting yourself first.

# Solar Plexus Chakra

Sometimes,
You find yourself in the middle of nowhere,
And sometimes,
In the middle of nowhere,
You find yourself.
www.behappy.me

The solar plexus energy will establish and define you as an individual. It will help you to know and honour yourself.

Self-definition requires boundaries. If a person does not know who they are, they may not recognise where their boundaries begin and end. In defining your own boundaries, you are more able to appreciate the boundaries of others. In not knowing your own boundaries, you may not be able to recognise those of others, and be intrusive without even realising it.

The solar plexus energy also introduces you to choices, confirming that you always had them, even if you didn't realise you did. Your whole being will be energised when you choose to honour yourself above all else.

Putting yourself first may not be clearly understood by those around you and explained as selfish, but it is essential to your future health and wellbeing.

Others who are not on a conscious journey of self-discovery may not give you permission to take this next step to self. They have depended on you to give them security and keep them safe. They have used you in their power games and dramas, so they would not have time to look more deeply at what life is intrinsically about. You may find resistance all around you.

As you try to analyse the implications of putting yourself first, logic may try to convince you that the cost of this giant leap to self is too high a price to pay. In distancing from unhealthy emotional attachment as you define your individuality, you may feel as though a part of you has died.

The entrapment of what you should be doing could be cast like a net from every direction, but you are strong enough, committed enough and determined enough to continue.

## Related issues

Your relationship to you.
Your rules and integrity.
Personal boundaries.
Boundaries of others.
The martyr invades.
The victim allows.
Liking and honouring yourself.
Self-respect and self-esteem.
What you should be doing.
Imposed guilt.
Pressure to conform.
Gut feelings.
Chaos.

## Healing the Solar Plexus Chakra

### Honour your boundaries and rules

Identify your personal boundaries. You may discover that you have no boundaries at all and others walk all over you with their demands and expectations. You may think you give to others when in reality, they blatantly take from you.

Some barriers may need to come down. You may have built brick walls around yourself to keep everyone out. You may only feel safe when you hold others at a distance.

Know yourself. Respect your boundaries.

Stop listening to other people and voices in your head telling you what you should be doing. Everything you are told you should do carries with it guilt, and guilt is nothing more than pressure from an outside source to make you conform. It is an emotion cast upon you to try to force you to change your priorities.

Acknowledge the necessity of putting yourself first. It is not selfish. It is essential.

## The martyr takes power from another

The martyr is often fulfilling a need within themselves, as they take power from another without consent.

They take responsibility for others because they don't believe that others have the courage, strength, wisdom or constitution to deal with a given situation.

The martyr thinks:
You are not strong enough, smart enough, well enough, tough enough, stoic enough; therefore I must do it for you whether you want me to or not.

The martyr can take away the pain and discomfort of a self-created lesson in the life of another because they don't like pain and suffering themselves. It is much easier to intervene and suffer themselves than to watch someone they love go through difficult times.

The martyr must learn to honour and respect the boundaries, choices and framework that others have set up for themselves to learn their own lessons. They must learn to offer support but not interfere and manipulate the consequence.

The martyr needs to say, "You have chosen a difficult lesson. Let me help you with it," without taking it from them.


## The victim gives their power to another

For whatever reason, the victim is afraid to take control and accept responsibility for their actions. Consciously or unconsciously they hand their power over to someone else, be it another person, circumstance or God.

The victim says:
I am not responsible. You are to blame. It's not my fault. I can't do it. Someone else did it to me. It always happens to me. Why does God let this happen?

As long as you afford control of a given event to another, you are giving your power away and are a victim in some form or other.

If someone else has created the circumstances, then a victim is powerless to make any changes because someone is doing something to them. Only when you acknowledge that you are responsible for something, do you have the power to change it.

The victim needs to learn not to dissolve or weaken the boundaries between themselves and another, and let the other person take on a problem that isn't theirs in the first place.

People all fall in and out of victimhood on a daily basis. Some only visit momentarily. Others choose to stay much longer. Being aware of your visits helps you to move on quickly, and learn from the experience.

## Chaos before order

Ilya Prigogine was a Russian-born Belgian who worked in the field of physical chemistry. For his pioneering work in non-equilibrium thermodynamics, he was awarded the Nobel Prize in Chemistry in 1977. Prigogine proved his hypothesis that *order emerges not in spite of chaos but because of it,* that evolution and growth are the inevitable product of open systems slipping into temporary chaos and then reorganising at higher levels of complexity.[1]
   As humans, we are part of the open system.

Next time your life is in chaos, remember that you are reorganising to a higher level of functioning. Growth cannot happen without it. Understanding this vital principle could enable someone to look at the chaos of all life in a different way. Chaos must happen otherwise higher order is not possible.
   Chaos pushes to the fore what isn't working so it can rearrange at a higher level of functioning.

The problem is that because we don't like our lives to be disturbed, we try to disperse the chaos before it reaches the point of transformation.
   Therefore, you must fall into temporary chaos before reorganising at a higher level of complexity.
How long the temporary chaos lasts is up to you.

## In summary

Give yourself permission to change.
Tell others you are changing but don't ask for their approval.
Clarify your personal boundaries.
Dismantle the brick walls that need to go.

---

[1] *(Thresholds of the Mind, Bill Harris, Centerpointe Research Institute, 2002)*

Make rules that honour you and your needs.
Get to know yourself without judgment.
Get to like and respect yourself.
Develop self-loyalty.
Be honest with yourself.
Keep the promises you make to yourself.
Be a person of integrity and let your actions match your beliefs and words.
Discover old beliefs that don't support and value your self-worth.
Treat yourself as your own best friend.
Take time out and relax.

## The Challenge

To put yourself first and not feel guilty.
To keep the promises you make to yourself.
To set your own rules.

# Worksheet

## Personal rules
- What are some of your personal rules?
- What promises have you made to yourself and not kept?

## The martyr
- Is there anyone you felt you had to save because you didn't believe that they could do something on their own?

- Whose boundaries do you invade, or have you invaded, without invitation?

## The victim
- What are your vulnerable areas, places where you feel you have little or no control; where someone else takes over?

## Chaos

Think of a time of chaos.

- What did it rearrange which subsequently allowed your life to function at a higher level?

- In retrospect, what was the best thing that ever happened to you, but you couldn't see it at the time?

In stating your personal rules, you set your boundaries and define who you are. In knowing your own boundaries, you are more likely to recognise and honour those of another. Resisting the temptation of taking the chaos of another upon yourself, you allow others to live out the scenarios they have set up for themselves to learn and evolve.

In understanding the purpose of chaos, you allow what is not functioning at its highest level to rearrange and become more productive.

As you enter into the energy of the heart chakra, you are happy to trust its guidance and follow your intuition. You are no longer controlled by patterns and beliefs from the past; you do not seek security in a source outside yourself, and you are comfortable with who you are becoming.

The heart is like the bridge between your lower and higher self. It connects the physical aspects of who you are to the spiritual ones. It asks you to move away from the known and comfortable, and trust the knowing that leads you.

# Heart Chakra

Who I am
is no longer challenged by
who I think I am
Glenda Hodge

The energy of the heart chakra beckons you to celebrate who you are. You have reached the point in your evolution where you know, without any doubt, who you are, and what your life is about. There is no emotion or thought attached to knowing. It just is.

A vibrant heart chakra merges logic, emotions and basic instincts to an indefinable knowing, a knowing that urges you to follow. You no longer need to understand everything, and you are no longer are controlled by emotions. You simply know. And that knowing will lead you safely wherever you go.

Everything is embraced, as forgiveness is transformed to gratitude. You understand there was never anything to forgive, for everything was your own creation to learn about yourself. Everything has always been on your terms.

You expand with gratitude for the person you were, the person you are and the person you are becoming. You are touched by the perfection of all that is. You know your life is exactly where it is meant to be. As you celebrate the gift of yourself, you cannot help but celebrate the gift of others.

The knowing energy of your heart is the catalyst that will push you forward, and help you to manifest a life of choice rather than one of unrelated circumstance.

You are not afraid to love. You open your heart to others. You invite them to share your great treasure: yourself.

## Related issues

Knowing without understanding.
Trusting the wisdom of your own heart to guide you.

49

Joy and happiness.
Compassion and gratitude.
Love, hate and forgiveness.
Conditional and unconditional love.
Self-expression.
Self-acceptance.
No longer having to prove yourself.

## Healing the Heart Chakra

### The dilemma of forgiveness versus the challenge of gratitude

Dilemma is described as a choice between a difficult or undesirable alternative. So the dilemma attached to forgiveness could be the undesirable alterative of gratitude.

Forgiveness is only a dilemma when you look at the material result of a physical event.
From a higher perspective everything is the way it is meant to be.
While in essence there may be nothing to forgive, gratitude may evolve slowly, if at all.

Dilemma: Do I forgive my primary caregivers and early teachers because they did not supply my perceived needs, or do I extend them gratitude for the situations they helped me create so that I could learn positives and strengths about myself?

Dilemma: Do I forgive those who wielded power and authority over me, or do I extend them gratitude because they showed me that power and authority were available to anyone who would embrace them as their own?

Dilemma: Do I forgive those who challenged me and appeared to deliberately annoy and aggravate me, or do I extend gratitude to them because they were reflecting back to me that part of myself that needed my attention?

Dilemma: Do I forgive those who abandoned and left me, or do I extend them gratitude because they created the space for me to be alone, and in my aloneness have the opportunity to recognise my strengths and get to know and love myself?

If I need to forgive someone, then I have concluded that they have done something to me.

Acceptance puts me on a higher plane to them. They have still done something to me but I will rise above it and accept it.

Gratitude acknowledges that there was nothing to forgive, for I invited the lesson into my life to evolve.


## The apology meditation

This meditation is very meaningful when you can close your eyes and listen to it being read. If that is not the case, read it slowly, pondering on the words, and allowing feelings to rise before continuing.

*There is nothing but love, only sometimes it comes in a package we don't recognize.*[2]

That statement being true, then everything that is done to you and everyone else is love.
There is nothing but love.

Think of a person who owes you an apology.
Imagine they are standing before you.
Now ask that person to forgive you.
Notice how you feel as you say the words…… Please forgive me.

Ask that person to forgive you because you have judged them as doing something to you, when in fact they were doing something for you.

Ask that person to forgive you because you have either forgotten, or not understood the role they were playing in your evolution.

Ask that person to forgive you because on some level of your consciousness you invited and agreed to the lesson. It was time for you to address something, and you needed them to help you to begin the process.

And think for a moment…….
What did you need to learn about yourself by inviting such a situation into your life?

And once again…..
Notice the person before you.

---

[2] John Demartini

Notice how you feel.

And remember......
the world you encounter is your reflection
and
love and gratitude are the keys to empowerment and change.

Love embraces.
Gratitude transforms.
Wisdom heals.

## In summary

Make choices that bring you joy and happiness.
Express your creativity.
Be grateful for your perceived failures, for they bring compassion.
Your inner guidance will never lead you astray.
Stop finding fault with yourself.
Forgive yourself for your perceived failings.
Accept compliments.
Observe what conditions you attach to your love.
Don't cling to those you love, let them go free.
Distance yourself a little from your logic and emotions, and know all is well.

## The Challenge

To be grateful for all things.
To change forgiveness to gratitude.
To trust your inner guidance even when it seems illogical.

# Worksheet

## Apology
- How did you initially feel when asked to forgive someone you believed had wronged you?

## How you felt
- How did you feel after you considered that you gave permission on some level of your consciousness?

## Wisdom verses logic
- When did you follow the knowing of your heart, even though it may have been illogical?

## Following your heart
- What is the wisdom of your heart asking you to do at present?

As you embrace all of your life experiences, and understand that everything is on your terms, gratitude transforms you. As you realise that forgiveness is simply another step to gratitude, you are free. As you follow the knowing of your heart, without logic or conditions, you take the easier road to your purpose and potential.

If you are not guided by the knowing of your heart, your throat chakra energy will be stifled and blocked by an imbalance between and logic, gut feelings and survival instincts as these three battle for dominance. As long as the battle continues, the throat is powerless to create anything by conscious positive choice.

When the energy of the throat flows freely, you are able to accept responsibility for everything that presents in your life. As your journey moves closer to the crown, you understand that everything is your creation, and on your own terms. Therefore, you can change it.

# Throat Chakra

When you think everything is someone else's fault,
you will suffer a lot.
Dalai Lama

The throat chakra energy enables you to express your innermost authentic self and claim your innate ability to create. It empowers you to speak up, manifest your beliefs and thoughts, and transform your life.

This chakra holds the energy for creating your own life circumstances through conscious choice, rather than existing within unexplained chaos. Underpinning the power of your thoughts and words is responsibility: a key issue of this chakra.

Before you can consciously draw to yourself circumstances of your choice, you need to accept responsibility for what is already there. If you are not the one responsible, then it follows that someone is doing something to you, and you are powerless. When you know you have created something, you also know you have the power to change it.

Another important issue that empowers the throat chakra to create by conscious choice is staying present to where you are. The only place is *here* and the time is *now*. Many people are not able to live in a *here and now* reality. We all take short trips away from time to time, but for the greater part, we need to stay there if we hope to create a lifestyle of choice.

The throat chakra is a pivot point: where past meets future, and head confronts heart.

The energy is negated by living in the past where the good old days were so much better, or oscillating to the future where everything will improve once something has changed.

## Related issues

Responsibility.
Empowerment.
Speaking up
Creating your own reality by conscious choice.
Being grateful for what you have already created.
Battle between the logic, gut feelings and survival instinct.
Living in the past.
Projecting to the future.
Living in the present.

## Healing the Throat Chakra

### I am responsible, Ho'oponopono

*If we can accept that we are the sum total of all past thoughts, emotions, words, deeds and actions and that our present lives and choices are coloured or shaded by this memory bank of the past, then we begin to see how a process of correcting or setting aright can change our lives, our families and our society[3].*

Ho'oponopono (ho-o-pono-pono) is an ancient Hawaiian practice of reconciliation and forgiveness.

This ancient practice brings with it an invitation to take full responsibility for everything that has ever happened to you. While at the level of logic that principle can make little or no sense, at a deeper level of knowing, it is a very freeing concept to embrace.

Experiences are created in one of two ways.
We connect to a memory. Good or bad memories are equally limiting because they both come from the past.
We allow divine inspiration to guide us. Intuition is imaginative and powerful as it flows directly from a higher source.

Ho'oponopono is not about analysing or examining anything. It is about letting go of memories, because the memories that are running in the

---

[3] Morrnah Nalamaku Simeona, recognised as a native Hawaiian Kahuna and gifted healer. She developed a modified version of the traditional Hawaiian forgiveness and reconciliation process of Ho'oponopono, and was recognised by the State of Hawaii as a Living Treasure in 1983.

subconscious dictate how a person interprets a given situation, and what they are seeing and experiencing.

People who show up in your reality share memories with you. By erasing a particular shared memory you change the reality for yourself and the other, because you and the other are all part of the One.

Ho'oponopono teaches that the only enemy is the memory that is currently playing. This can be experienced as judgment, anger, resentment, hate or other negative emotions. Bringing love and gratitude to anything will transform it.

Therefore, to the memory that replays anger, you might say, "I love you. I'm sorry. Forgive me. Thank you."

Going within and clearing those memories can change the experiences we are having.

When the memories are erased you are in a place of freedom, where you can be moved by inspiration.

When there are no memories surfacing which bring with them bias, behavioural patterns or unresolved issues, you are free. It is in this void, space and emptiness that you will find inspiration and divine guidance.


## Gratitude transforms

Choosing thoughts of forgiveness and gratitude transform painful circumstances, memories and judgments to love, allowing creative solutions and possibilities to present themselves. And, while the circumstances may not change, your perception will change, and that is what makes the difference.

Some time ago, I remember going to a lot of trouble to choose a gift for someone. She opened it, looked at it, and then proceeded to tell me that she would never use it, and gave it back to me. I was devastated. So, you might not be surprised to know that I didn't give her another thing for a long, long time. I felt that there was no gratitude for the effort made, only criticism because it was deemed to be not useful.

By creating our own life circumstances, we give ourselves a gift; a precious gift that once opened and appreciated, will be of great value to us.

But like my friend in the story, we can be quick to judge the gift as useless, and dismiss it.

In bringing love and gratitude to our life circumstances, no matter how painful, useless or unnecessary we think they are, we see them in a different light. Gratitude changes our perception. It helps us to see past the obvious, and discover the hidden treasure. When we are happy to accept and lovingly open the gifts we give to ourselves, they keep coming. It is like fast-tracking our potential and growth.

When we are critical and unthankful, the gifts won't necessarily stop coming to us, but we will take so long to appreciate their worth, that we slow down our progress along our journey through life.

## Stilling the mind

If the place of empowerment is the *here and now*, mindfulness, mantras and meditations may help you find it.

### Mindfulness

Mindfulness is described as a state of being in the present, accepting things for what they are without judgement. It is the ability to live consciously by bringing your attention to the present experience.

*Mindfulness is simply being aware of what is happening right now without wishing it were different.*

*Enjoying the pleasant without holding on when it changes (which it will).*

*Being with the unpleasant without fearing it will always be this way (which it won't).* [4]

In accepting the reality of your life, your mind is calm and at peace, not searching for answers, or seeking to solve the problems of the world. The still mind is open to divine intervention which can arrive at inappropriate times, in unexpected places, in unusual ways. Only a still mind will capture its wisdom, as the noise and clutter of randomness can often drown it out.

### Mantras

Mantras are empowered words, verses, phrases or sounds, repeated in a spiritual context, that help to focus within.

In giving the mind something uplifting to focus on, it discourages it from busyness and inquiry. The mind cannot do two things at once. If it is focusing within by repeating something, it isn't able to chatter at the same time. By focusing on an uplifting verse, quote or sound, the mind isn't able to worry or become anxious. It may drift away, but the more you bring it back, the less it eventually wanders.

---

[4] James Baraz. https://www.awakeningjoy.info/teacher.html

Singing or saying a holy mantra can bring you to, and anchor you in, the *here and now*, the only place where you can change the circumstances of your self-created reality.

Mantras can also be in the form of a drawing, to ponder and contemplate. Focusing on a spiritual image can bring you to a place of empowerment, as it stills the mind, and allows space for inspiration to flow.

## Meditation

Over the years, many people have asked me if I mediate. My reply is always the same. What do you mean by 'meditate'?

I've always thought of meditation as being present to what you are doing, much like mindfulness. While I rarely, if ever, sit with my eyes closed and repeat a mantra, focus on my breath or visualise something, I know such practices can be a very effective way of reaching a meditative state for many people.

There was a time when I spent many hours in prayer, but that wasn't really stilling my mind and listening. It was more about talking on my part.

I did find that speaking in a language that I didn't learn or understand had a noticeable effect on my mind. Some people called it star language, others referred to it as speaking in tongues, but whatever was happening, I think it confused the mind so much, the mind somehow decided that it didn't want to be involved, and kept out. Somehow, the strange words and quiet mind allowed insight to appear from nowhere.

Some of my most inspiring insights into life have come to me when my eyes were wide open, and I was working on someone's feet, totally focused, present to the moment and to what I was doing.

The space and emptiness might only last a short while, but the impact it delivers can be life changing.

## In summary

Speak with truth and integrity, as it is the most powerful tool you can yield.

Make your own choices, and accept responsibility for what they bring you. Let others be responsible for their own choices.

Create from divine guidance rather than old controlling memories.

Recognise the beliefs and thought patterns that have shaped your life experiences to date.

Notice the words you use to describe your circumstances.

Is there a connection between what you say and what appears in your life? Identify recurring patterns.

Visiting the past is one thing; living there is another.

Don't be too quick to crave the future; it may not happen as you expect it to.
The place is here, and the time is now.
Find a balance between the heart and head.


## The Challenge

I am responsible.
I created it; therefore, I can change it.
Nothing happens to me without my permission on some level of my consciousness.

## Worksheet

### The void
- How do you reach your void; your inner space that is free and empty, and ready for inspiration to show itself?

### In retrospect
- Remember a time when you tried to figure out a solution to a difficult situation, and at the last minute, you came up with a solution that was so brilliant, you even surprised yourself.

### Memories
- What memories constantly replay in your mind?

- What situations could these be attracting to you?

**Gratitude**
- What situations do you find it difficult to bring gratitude to?

- Which of your self-created gifts to yourself are you not able to embrace and open with love?

As you quiet your mind and become open to inspiration, you are guided by a wisdom that is past understanding.

As you love your creations, you see their value. As you accept responsibility for your creations, you can change them.

As you send love to the memory of the person you once were, you free that part of yourself that is stuck and holding you back.

As you follow the wisdom of your heart, and discover the creative power of the throat, you understand that something or someone far greater than your conscious mind can imagine is present.

As you flow with this creative energy and open your mind to possibility, you may discover realms and perspectives that once were never contemplated.

The third eye energy is the doorway to all that is not held within your conscious memory. It is a portal to higher consciousness and enlightenment.

May you enter with excitement and expectation.

# Third Eye Chakra

We can easily forgive a child who is afraid of the dark;
The real tragedy of life is when men are afraid of the light.
Plato

The energy of the third eye will take you past the physical, the logical and the explainable to an understanding of the metaphysical, the paranormal and the esoteric.

This energy asks you to re-evaluate your beliefs, and reconsider life from a higher perspective. It invites you to open your mind and pursue possibility, be comfortable with the unexplained, and offer no judgment as positive and negative are an intrinsic factor in the physical reality.

It challenges you to look again at everything you have come to know, believe and value through the vision and clarity of something greater than your logical mind.

The third eye invites you to move through the three dimensions of the physical world into the realm of the unknown. It is the doorway to other dimensions and life forms apart from those you can see and explain. It opens your psychic pathways, allowing you to experience and understand spiritual phenomena, and connects you to the insights of the spirit world with its many profound secrets.

A empowered third eye gives you perception beyond your ordinary sight as auras become visible, out of body experiences reveal you are more than just a physical being, and precognition as the future reveals itself in unexpected ways.

How far you wish to open your third eye is your choice.

The world is evolving and we are evolving with it. Times are changing, and we are swept along. The shift is from the Age of Pisces – an age where we listened to wisdom from outside of ourselves and followed in trust – to the Age of Aquarius. This new age is connected to the mind and understanding. No longer do we have to follow another in trust. We have the ability to listen to our own inner wisdom and forge our own pathway, because we have connected with something far greater than the physical to guide us.

## Related issues

Seeing from a different perspective.
Making something right or wrong.
Judging or allowing.
Psychic phenomena and abilities.
Other dimensions.
Closed mind.
New ideas.

## Healing the Third Eye Chakra

### Opening a closed mind

If a person hears something that aligns with their value system, they will usually open their mind and listen to what is being said. If it doesn't fit with what they believe and value, they may well ignore it.

The wise person is alert to new information that will stretch and benefit them, even if it is outside their comfort zone, and even though it may take them some years to process and apply it.

A closed mind likes to understand, appreciates logic, and needs explanations. It is challenged by the intuitive knowing of the heart, as there is no sound reasoning attached. It fears the unknown as it doesn't know if it will be able to maintain control.

The closed mind can be quite irrational when you are trying to introduce changes based on inner guidance rather than logic. It can feel it is losing control, and needs to fight to the death to maintain the status quo.

When you open your mind to something new, and make radical changes, it affects every part of you.

Your inner child, who lives in your memories, plays an important role in any denial or irrational response. Rather than drag them along, kicking and screaming, why not comfort and reassure them that all is well?

Why not substitute a teddy bear for that part of you who is frightened, and give reassurance that change will be safe, bring no harm and might even end up being exciting. You could even stroke your surrogate teddy bear lovingly, as you dispel the fears of your inner child.

The rejection or negativity that arises when you open your mind to something new and different is most often not directly related to the issue at hand. It is simply bringing up some unresolved issues that need to be addressed. The current problem is not the real problem. It is simply redirecting you to something else that needs attention.

A closed mind will judge something to be right or wrong according to the person's value system.
Right judgment is no judgment.
No judgment is allowing.

When someone chooses to focus solely on those things that primarily support what they already believe and value, they may risk developing a narrow focus on life, living with tunnel vision, and limiting their potential.
In letting go of the fear that holds your mind fixed and closed, and becoming open to new concepts, you are not being disloyal to what has gone before. New information is constantly around you. It is a positive trait to process anything new, rather than dismiss it unexplored.

Change is a constant. Anything that doesn't change in some way is usually dead. Don't let your mind ring your death knell by refusing to consider the unfamiliar.


## Opposites are essential to definition

Opposites (polarities) are essential for definition and experience.
One is neither right nor wrong. They simply are.
A person cannot know what up is without knowing what down is.
They can't define cold if there is no hot.
This is not saying that hot, for example, is good and cold is bad.
Both are necessary for either experience.

> **Somewhere over the centuries the science of the physical reality (positive and negative)**
> **became confused and intertwined with**
> **the value system of a particular group or culture (good/bad, right/wrong).**

Morality and justice are rules and values devised and orchestrated to protect society. These can change or be changed at will, depending on culture, beliefs and who is in charge. What one culture believes to be right could be judged wrong by another. What someone said was good, another could say was bad. Each person has their own value system that dictates their choices. Everyone doesn't play by the same rules.

**Right and wrong are relative to a value system.**
**A value system is relative to the belief system of a particular person, group or culture.**
**Therefore right and wrong are not definites.**
**They are relative to something or someone else.**

Imagine a see-saw. To have *good* outweighing *bad* is equally out of balance as to have *bad* out-weighting *good*. As each becomes less extreme, the see-saw begins to come into balance.

At the point where the see-saw is in perfect balance, and neither side is favoured, there is a portal, which opens to universal light and understanding; a portal so positioned that it can only be found at the exact point of no judgments, where good and bad are equally weighted, and once again become the positive and negative polarity essential for any experience and definition.

I am not saying that this concept doesn't bring with it challenges. Of course, it does. But, what I am saying is that other philosophies bring challenges to their beliefs as well.

If God loves everyone equally, then whose side was He on in wars where millions of people were killed? If God protects us, why are young children killed by drunken drivers, or sexually abused, and why do mothers of young children have to die?

Every philosophy or religion brings its own challenges, be they Christian, New Age or anything else.

If positive and negative simply are, then maybe life is that way also. It simply is. There will always be that which can't be understood or explained.

As the see-saw comes back to perfect balance both sides rise at the same time. As group consciousness rises and the world becomes more aware, so does its opposite.

Maybe that is part of the reason for such unrest in the world today.


## In summary

Open your mind to possibility, and look with vision not focus.
Acknowledge the positive and negative balance of the physical universe.
Right and wrong are not definites. They are relative to a specific value.
Refuse to judge, allow things to be as they are.

Refuse to judge yourself, and you will learn not to judge others.
Open your mind to your own psychic gifts, everyone has them.
Psychic abilities are your own personal short cuts which bypass the long and tedious labours of the mind and logic.
Consider life forms and realities outside of what you can see and explain.
Look past the obvious.

## The Challenge

To change good/bad, right/wrong back to positive and negative and refuse to judge.
To open your mind to possibility.

# Worksheet

## The closed mind
- What areas, ideas and concepts do you close your mind to?

- If fear is the cause or contributes to your closed mind, what are you afraid of?

## The open mind
- What ideas and concepts have you discovered but not yet explored?

## Mysteries
- How do you deal with the unexplainable and the physically impossible?

## Other value systems
- What are some things deemed good or bad in the value system of another that you disagree with?

## Which value system takes preference?
- When value systems differ, which one should receive preference?

## Where do some people fit in?
- Where do terrorists fit into a value system that sees positive and negative as equals, and makes no judgments?

## Positive and negative
- If you changed right and wrong back to positive and negative, how would it affect your approach to certain people in your life?

What a person values is very precious to them. They protect it, and in certain circumstances are prepared to die for it. However, we don't all value the same things. Each of us has our own personal value system, and many come into conflict.

The energy of the third eye invites us not to judge what another values, but to allow it. In many ways this may seem like an almost intolerable request, but we are moving away from the physical world as we know it into a realm we may not be familiar with, where possibility exists, and definites are difficult to establish.

As you open your mind to concepts that you may have once dispelled without a second thought, and find value in places where you may have refused to visit, you will change. As a result, you may become distant from some, and become closer to others, but the most important thing is to stay true to what you have discovered, even though it will bring with it new challenges and trials.

There are many reasons why a person might close their mind to ideas that they are uncomfortable with or can't explain. May fear not be one of them.

As you move through your third eye energy towards your final step to the crown, you are asked to put aside judgments and simply allow life to be. You are invited to consider what could be challenging possibilities, as they may not fit into any of your current beliefs, rules or patterns. As you allow the energy of your third eye to embrace you, logic may disappear and explanations become obscure.

You are being asked to move into unchartered waters with openness, and to look from a new perspective. The vision may be confronting if you are still holding firm to the security of the past.

# Crown Chakra

Earth's crammed with heaven
And every common bush afire with God
And only he who sees takes off his shoes
The rest sit round and pluck blackberries
Elizabeth Barrett Browning


The crown chakra is the doorway to your innate spiritual nature. Its purpose is to dissolve the ego and unite with Spirit. It seeks to break down the barriers of illusion, so you can understand the oneness of all creation.

The Universe and all that it contains is perfect.

Life is unfolding as it should.

There are no mistakes, accidents or coincidences.

As you allow its energy to transcend from the higher realms into your physical reality, it has the ability to transform you. As you embrace what you know in Spirit, and apply it to your everyday life in a practical way, you will understand the meaning of grounding.

As the energy of the crown descends down through every cell of your body, you become humbly aware of the opportunity it brings with it for change.

The smallness of the logical mind is opened to possibility.

The insignificant voice speaks with authority and creates a lifestyle of choice.

You follow your heart as it guides you with knowing and wisdom.

You honour and respect yourself.

You acknowledge all those around you as your teachers.

You are grateful for every physical experience because you understand that it was all on your terms.

Embrace the reality of your own life with gratitude, and try not to escape. Connect to your spiritual essence, and allow it to transform your day-to-day experiences.

The crown makes sense of the past, shows hope for the future, brings understanding to the chaos, and casts peace and calmness wherever it moves. You are left with a sense of knowing that all is well.


## Related issues

Unity and Oneness.
Illusion.
Universal guidance.
Closure.
Transformation.
Self-mastery.
Ego.
Control.
Trust and vulnerability.


## Healing the Crown Chakra


### God, the gift of divinity

When I name, I define; when I define, I exclude.
To speak of God, I may exclude those who say Universe.
To use the word Him, I may offend those who choose Her.
To explore religion I may ostracise those who embrace other philosophies.
To talk of the occult I may lose those who do not understand its essence.

Ultimately, whichever words I choose, they all mean the same.
There is only One, who has no parts, no divisions, no sections.
If nothing is outside of God, then everything is God.
Everything is a valid expression of God: from the highest expression of the human condition to the lowest.
There can be no exception.

## My essence surpasses logic and understanding: I am God

The Christian church teaches that we are created in the image of God. Being told, "You are God!" is something altogether different.

The first time I heard the statement was at the conference of the International Council of Reflexologists in Rome in September 2001. I hadn't come across that concept before, and the words were spoken with such power and authority that I thought I may have misunderstood what had been said.

My first response was utter disbelief, almost anger, but a seed had been planted which would flower in due time.

I came to believe that we are all One, irrespective of what name we use to address It. I also came to believe that everything in the universe, including the human condition, is the experience of that One, often called God.

Knowing is one thing. Experience is another.

I likened my understanding to a piece of chocolate cake. I could look at the cake, and know it would taste delicious, but the experience of eating the cake was something altogether different. In the experience there had to be *something other than* the chocolate cake, so that I could define the chocolate cake and appreciate its unique qualities.

I eventually came to realise that the *something other than* was the illusion necessary for any definition, as every experience can only be had in relation to something else. Apparent separation was the only way to define and identify a specific experience, especially when it came to the human experience of God. Polarity or opposites were equally important to identify and name the quality of such experience.

I believe that the relative Universe is God in experience, and I am here to take part. Joining in the human experience of God brought with it the illusion of separation. The illusion being, that the human condition is separate to God when in reality it is not.

In realising that the only possible passage to any experience is through definition, one begins to understand that the illusion of separation was the only means the human condition had to be part of the God experience.

In the physical reality, by embodying an ego and defining who I am, I am simultaneously identifying who I am not.

In the spiritual reality there is no separation from God or anyone else. Everything was, is and will be part of the One. It cannot be any other way.

## In summary

Know that the Universe and all that it contains is perfect.
Life is unfolding as it should.
There are no mistakes, accidents or coincidences.
Trust Spirit to guide you.
Try not to escape the disillusionment, disappointment and confusion of the world.
Trust what you don't understand, and wisdom will eventually show herself.
Take absolute control away from your mind, logic and ego.
Accept the reality of your own life with gratitude.
Some things must end or close to allow something new and refreshing to enter.
To expand your consciousness, you must visit your horizons.
You are not your ego; you are something far greater.
Know the difference between a boundary that protects you, and one that contains you.
Your ego defines you, but it does not separate you from Source.

## The Challenge

Separation from Source is an illusion. You are God.
Trust your spiritual beliefs and allow them to transform your daily experiences.

## Worksheet

### Greater than ourselves
- How do you describe that which is often called God?

### Illusions
- What are the illusions in your life that are disguised as facts?

### Your life path
- After all your consideration, why do you think you are here, and where is your current pathway leading you?

In this final chakra worksheet, you are asked to ponder, once again, on what life is about, your innate essences, and the reasons you are here.

As you ascend towards the crown and view your life from a different perspective, you begin to understand all that may have made little sense in the past. While much in life can make little sense at the time, in retrospect, it can be obvious. From your higher point of view, every piece of the puzzle fits perfectly. You look back with gratitude, and as your focus moves away from a specific experience, you realise that it is only a tiny part of a much larger picture, a picture you can now appreciate because you have taken a step back, and become the observer.

# A Meditation

Chakra energy takes us through a transformation from our most basic primal instincts in the base chakra to our highest spiritual self in the crown.

Reversing the process, it brings back what we discover in the spiritual realm, and keeps us grounded and practical in everyday life. It applies a higher perspective and a greater understanding to our lives, bringing a calmness of purpose and a knowing that everything is exactly where it is meant to be at any given moment.

As we open to this energy and flow, we might describe ourselves as growing.

As we apply this spiritual knowledge and energy to our everyday life in a practical way, we might describe ourselves as grounded.

When we block the information coming to us through these energy vortexes, we may think of ourselves as stuck.


In a quiet and peaceful place, read slowly, ponder the words and allow their wisdom to refresh you.


As you focus on your crown chakra you feel your connection with Spirit. You surrender, for you know that you are being guided by something or someone far greater than yourself. You embrace the perfection of all things and follow in trust the pathway before you.

As your third eye opens, you gaze with vision rather than focus. And as the logic of the mind quietens, you are ready to consider all possibilities and know that one is neither good nor bad, but simply part of the illusion necessary for the experience.

The throat chakra asks you to take responsibility for your life and all it contains. And as the insignificant voice speaks with authority, you are empowered to create a lifestyle of your choice. You release the past, withdraw from the future and immerse in the power of the present.

You embrace the knowing of the heart for here you find wisdom; wisdom that unfolds with love and gratitude. And this knowing of the heart is more powerful than logic, more stable than emotions, and calmer than your survival instincts. This knowing is to be honoured and followed lest it be stolen away by your unconscious fears that bind you.

As the energy of Spirit connects with your solar plexus you know who you are. You define your own rules, honour your needs and reinstate your personal boundaries without guilt or pressure. It's alright if others don't understand your new found strength. It's alright if others don't understand that you must put yourself first. It's alright if others call you selfish. In time they will reap the benefits of your changes, but for now, everything is alright.

And as the power of Spirit touches your sacral chakra, you understand the meaning of relationships. Nothing was ever done to you. It was only ever done for you, with your consent on some level of your consciousness. You understand that everyone is your teacher; power-games only surface when you forget that you gave permission to someone to teach you something about yourself.

And as the energy of the crown imbues the base chakra, it brings with it transformation.
You recognise the survival instincts that have dominated your life.
You are freed from beliefs that limit your potential.
You identify behavioural patterns that no longer serve your highest good.
You feel a sense of peace as you understand much of the unexplained pain the world suffers.
You are grateful for every experience you have ever had because you understand that it was all on your terms with your consent.

And as the energy of the crown is welcomed, it releases what is out-dated and puts to work in a practical way what you have always known in Spirit.
You feel safe, at home and grounded.


And so the cycle begins again.
You step into your future with optimism.
In awe of the power within.
Pondering your choices with hope and expectation.
Knowing all is well.

# Part II

## The Purpose of Pain

This section considers why some people need to be sick, the benefits of illness, and reasons not to get well. It also discusses why a specific health issue would present in a particular chakra area of the body or foot, and what message it is trying to convey.

Energy flow in the subtle body is as important as blood flow in the physical body, and while one is measurable and the other not, they are both vitally essential for optimum wellness. If blood flow through the body and to the heart is blocked or inhibited in any way, serious health problems can occur, sometimes resulting in death.

Blocked energy can have the same effect. While in essence energy is intangible, as it becomes blocked and changes form it can appear as a material or physical manifestation. As mentioned in the introduction, Albert Einstein has proven that energy and matter are interchangeable.

Energy needs to flow freely through the subtle body to maintain harmony and balance. Therefore, understanding what causes blockages and how to dissolve them are a vital part of the healing process.

In the physical body blockages to blood flow can occur in many ways. Plaque can build up in arteries, causing them to harden, reducing flow, resulting in the heart having to work harder. Aneurysms can rupture, causing haemorrhage. Blood can clot, starving cells of oxygen and causing them to die.

Just as blockages on the physical level affect optimum wellness, so do blockages on an energetic level. Emotions could be described as energy in motion. Therefore, suppressing emotions is one way to block energy. Refusing to follow a pathway that you know is for your higher good is another way to block your energy flow. Continuing to do something when you know that it doesn't serve your highest potential, keeps you stuck, brings disharmony, and blocks your ability to flow with life.

When a person refuses to reassess something in their life that isn't working, and refuses to consider alternatives and make any beneficial changes, their higher consciousness might come to their aid. Whatever it is that is blocking their journey may be emphasised in such a way that it can no longer be ignored. When energy is blocked it can cause problems in the physical body, by creating health issues.


In this section the focus is on certain health problems and the messages they are trying to convey. In understanding the basics of some diseases, parallels can be drawn with areas of life that need attention.

A summary of each body system can be found in Appendix I, and while these descriptions are basic and short, more information is available online. I would encourage the reader to gather information about the specific health problem without going into information overload, and then put it together with the other pieces you have gleaned in the process. In learning how to put random pieces of information together, you will paint a picture, which is not all that difficult to do. You will learn the process of finding your own answers, rather than having to ask someone else.

Other people – including me – are the scaffolding that supports you, until you are able to do it for yourself.

# Why am I sick?

Pain, sickness and disease are part of a complex web of inter-related issues on several levels: physical, mental, emotional and spiritual. They can manifest in many ways, have subtle hidden causes, and can show up in the most unexpected places.

On a physical level, pain and disease can manifest when a person continues to ignore the more subtle messages that the body is trying to bring to their attention.

Serious life-threatening diseases can be well established before they are diagnosed. There were most probably many clues along the way to let someone know that something wasn't working properly, but these could have been ignored. You can choose if and when you take notice of what your body and lifestyle are trying to tell you, but sometimes a response may not come until very late in the process, when the issue has transformed into matter, so dense, that it is described as irreparable.

There are many and varied reasons why people need to be sick. Not everyone wants to get better. Keeping in mind that on some level of your consciousness you allow, create or draw to yourself your life circumstance, let us consider why you might have allowed your physical body to fall into disharmony and what it is trying to tell you.


There are many answers to the question: *Why am I sick?*

One of the most common ones is that the disease was inherited. It runs in the family. The person didn't have a choice.

There is no disputing that a person inherits their genes, but science has proved that genes are influenced by environmental factors. There are two basic groups of environmental factors that influence a living organism. Firstly, there are the abiotic factors which are the non-living resources or physical conditions, such as soil pH, water, air, temperature and sunlight.

Then there are the biotic factors: the living things that have an effect. Availability or lack of food can result in starvation, over-eating, a limited variety of or unsuitable food choices. The presence of like species allows for empathy, being understood, support networks, belonging or being accepted and loved. Competitors bring forth striving, never being satisfied, and aggressive, challenging or relentless behaviour. Predators encourage defensive behaviour, allow no relaxation, encourage self-reliance and keep a person in fight or flight mode, always ready for battle. Parasites attach to a host and drain, exhaust and use their energy.

There are many known factors that affect genes.

Beliefs and subsequent thoughts are also a part of our everyday life, which makes them part of our environment as well.

If genes are influenced by environmental factors, is it not possible that thoughts and belief patterns could also contribute to the environmental factors that influence a gene?

A strongly held family belief that has been passed down through the generations could contribute to the ongoing presence of a particular disease in a particular family line.

Individual thinking and individual beliefs, apart from what the family line believes, could be a reason why one person in a family manifests something and another doesn't.

Another common answer to this question, especially when it is related to the flu or a virus is, "it's going around."

Everybody has got it, so it is inevitable that you will pick it up as well. Is this a self-creating thought pattern of the individual, or a consensus of group consciousness empowering what could be an epidemic in the community?

Religious people will often describe sickness as a trial sent from God to make them stronger. This would appear to be a contradiction. If God sent the sickness to make people stronger, and Jesus went around healing everyone, then they were working against each other.

Therefore, it would appear that sickness came from some other source.

There are also hidden, denied or disowned answers as to why people are sick.

Sickness can make someone the centre of attention, as people visit and talk to them. Lonely and elderly people no longer feel isolated when someone comes to see them regularly. They receive sympathy and empathy, something they may not receive if they are strong and independent.

When someone needs time out, a holiday, relaxation, a rest, or time to pursue a hobby, and won't follow through and arrange it for themselves, God/Universe/Higher Self can arrange it for them. In this case take care not

81

to say, "I need a break," as that is most probably what will happen: a broken leg or arm.

Not wanting to appear ungrateful is another hidden reason why people may need to be sick.

Some parents encourage their child/children to succeed in areas where they failed to achieve. A parent may have invested money and time into a child to develop a certain area/sport. Initially the child may have been interested and passionate, but there comes a time when the child may not want to continue. So as not to appear ungrateful, the child has an accident or develops an injury. The training has to stop.

Also, if someone owes a favour to another – and, for whatever reason, doesn't want to repay it – they won't be judged as ungrateful if they become sick.

When a person can't recognise boundaries, they may take on someone else's problems, thinking they are their own.

It's not uncommon for a child to take on the issues of a parent and manifest the consequences as a health problem. The issue really belongs to the parent, but the child is carrying the physical load.

In many areas of life, people carry responsibilities for others, weighing themselves down and eventually becoming sick. Often these people aren't able to put the heavy load down because they are driven to carry it by guilt.

Escape can be another disowned reason to be sick.

An accident or injury gets a person out of doing something they may not want to do or face up to. This can be a last minute unconscious avoidance plan. Ill health can be a very effective way to delay the inevitable or escape from it.

There are also philosophical answers to questions about sickness.

Death is an honourable way to leave.

It can be the answer for the peace-maker who may have suffered in silence for many years. It is a way to leave with dignity when a person has had enough. Death and illness can be a non-confrontational response for a person who keeps everything inside.

Terminal illness allows time to say goodbye.

When it is time to leave, an extended illness gives someone time to put things in order and possibly come to terms with death. It gives the family time to make adjustments. Sudden death can leave much unsaid or unresolved.

Illness or injury can be wake-up call.
Some people know their lifestyle isn't sustainable, but won't change. It's only after a serious illness or an accident that people may reassess their patterns and make the necessary readjustment. Often a major illness can stop someone in their tracks, keep them still, and give them time to think about what is important in life. It can be their second chance.

A person knows that they have done what they came to do.
Someone who is aware of their life purpose may know when they have finished what they came for, and that it is time to leave. For some people this may take many years. For others, it is accomplished in a very short period of time.
Jesus died around the age of thirty. From a religious perspective, he accomplished what he came to do. From a logical perspective, was his life wasted because it ended so early?
Miscarriages, still births or the death of a child can bring intense sorrow. It is not always possible to see a higher meaning through such sadness, but we are so much more than our physical bodies and our conscious memory. We are radiant beings of light, here on the earth, on our own terms, far surpassing the mind and its understanding. As your beliefs and theories are challenged, do you let them go, or search for reasons to uphold them?

Another philosophical explanation in regard to sickness and disability could be that a person is resolving issues from another lifetime.
Someone who is completely dependent on others could be balancing aggression in other lifetimes by doing no harm in this one. Disability could be the contract someone makes so as to be a teacher for their family or for society.
A child who stays a short time in this lifetime could have agreed to be a temporary support for another, or have agreed to help them set up a particular experience. If someone's contract is connected to unconditional love, then there would need to be circumstances to draw that out.

While there are reasons to be sick or have an accident, there are also reasons to stay sick. Looking deeply at life can often uncover a hidden agenda.

Compensation pay-outs are one reason why people need to stay sick or their injuries to show no improvements. Healing a workplace injury isn't conducive to optimum pay-outs.

Groups who are lobbying governments for funding in relation to specific conditions and medications may not want to acknowledge that the condition can be improved in other ways. Addressing the underlying problem and improving the physical issue in any way may negate the argument for funding. It can be preferable to lobby governments for funding of pharmaceuticals rather than deal with repressed issues that contributed to the problems in the first place.

The carer who is exhausted has a valid reason for staying sick. When the long-term carer gets sick, it is quite common that the person cared for improves, but only for the duration of the carer's illness. When the carer recovers, the symptoms of the person cared for reappear. After this pattern repeats several times, the carer knows what to expect. The carer knows that it is not in their best interest to stay well.

Illness and pain can be used to excuse bad or unacceptable behavior. Rudeness and bad temper are often blamed on a specific disease. If the person did some form of personal development work, they may find that the bad behavior has a deeper source which sickness conceals. Ill health could be the best option for an angry person, rather than having to look too deeply within at what is causing the anger in the first place.


After considering the reasons to be sick and the benefits of staying sick, a person may choose wellness, and begin to listen to the messages of the body, but the messages may have been ignored for so long that the physical damage is extensive and unable to be repaired as the person would hope for.

Understanding the messages of the body is no guarantee that a person will get better, as sickness and disease is a complex web of inter-related issues on several levels: physical, mental, emotional and spiritual.

It is well to your advantage to deal with issues and problems when they first appear, rather than ignore them until they escalate to a point where they can't be ignored any longer.

# Symptoms and disease

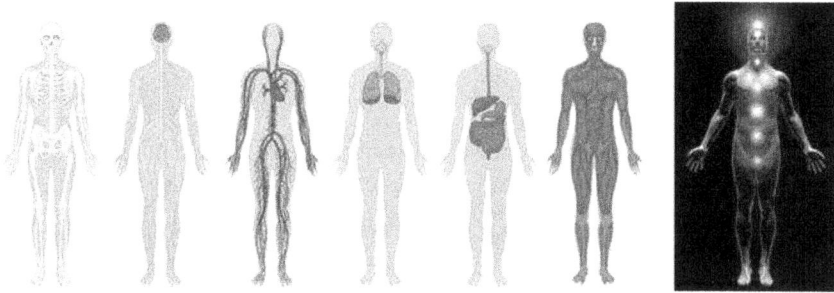

As sickness is a complex web of inter-related issues, you may need to consider several pieces of information before the puzzle begins to come together, and makes any sense.[5]

Identifying what issues sit in certain areas of our bodies can help to identify what is contributing to pain and discomfort in that particular area.

Subsequently, if there is pain and discomfort in a particular area of the body, knowing what issues reside there, can help to identify what is required to relieve it.

In deciphering the messages of the body, it is important to keep in mind:
* Specific lifestyle issues reside in specific parts of the body. Knowledge of the chakras makes it relatively easy to pinpoint which area or issue in your life needs some attention. This has already been discussed at length.

---

[5] Parts of the puzzle that may need to be considered are found in the Appendix. Discussion includes a basic overview of the twelve body systems, an alternative perspective on cancer, autoimmune disorders, infection and inflammation, and the difference between viruses and bacteria. Emotions of the organs are listed, as is the meaning of the left and right sides of the body.
Family beliefs and their contribution to illness, hereditary disease and chakra blockages and their resulting effects have already been discussed in detail. In deciphering the messages of the body and feet, it is important to take all of these factors into consideration.

- Each body system and its individual components have a unique function to perform. The most basic understanding of how the body works makes it relatively easy to parallel that knowledge to the metaphysical, and consider what the body is trying to tell you.
- Suppressed emotions hide in particular organs. Knowing which emotions sit in which organs makes it is relatively easy to identity what is being suppressed or denied.
- In realising that the left side of the body equates to all that is female and feminine, and the right to all that is male and masculine, it can be relatively easy to isolate who or what an issue could be associated with.
- Beliefs play an important role in what you manifest. Being aware of what you or your family believe about the symptom, sickness or disease may bring understanding to how thoughts contribute to a heredity disease.

In deciphering the messages of the feet, it is important to keep in mind:
The feet reflect the body. By knowing where your organs sit in your body, it is relatively easy to parallel that to their position on the feet, and understand which part of your body is under stress in some way when your feet are in pain in certain areas.

Other information to help solve the puzzle:
When did the problem begin?
What was happening in your life at the time?

# Base Chakra and the body

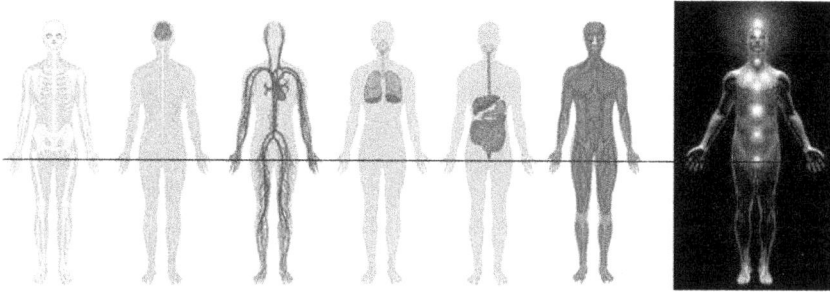

Areas of the body: coccyx, pelvic area, reproductive organs, sigmoid colon, bladder.
Pain, symptoms and disease that present in these areas of the body are related in some way to the family, tribe, group, religion or culture.


## Bladder Cancer

Cancer: You have lost your sense of identity. You don't know who you are or where you belong.
Bladder: Collects urine from the kidneys through the ureters, and stores it until it is expelled from the body. The collection process is slow, storage is temporary, but the toxins must leave the body.

Your sense of self, purpose and identity are associated with:
Holding something back, until you can hold it back no longer.
A process that is taking too long to finish off.
Being patient.
The need to release something but being unable to do so.
A toxic environment that you can't escape from.


## Coccyx injuries

When a bone is broken, splintered, squashed or fragmented, the message is related to something that has broken down, and needs to be restructured or rebuilt.

Problems with the tail bone are related to a need to restructure something within, or related to your tribe, family, culture, traditions or religion.

## Constipation

Constipation refers to bowel movements that are infrequent or hard to pass. The longer the residue is held on to, the more difficult it becomes to get rid of it. Chronic constipation can be easier to prevent than treat.

What else in life would have been easier to deal with at the time, rather than have to address the unpleasant results of delay?
What are you holding on to that is absolutely of no further use to you?
What are you struggling to let go of?
Needing outside help because you have let a given situation go on too long.
This situation didn't really need to become this painful.

## Diarrhoea

Diarrhoea occurs when residue moves through the bowel too quickly and fluid cannot be re-absorbed from the contents. Extra fluid can also be secreted into the bowel, causing the faeces to be very runny.

I just want to get rid of this.
The sooner this is out of my life the better.
Letting something go without learning or taking anything from it.
Needing to slow down a process.

## Prostate cancer

Cancer: You have lost your sense of identity. You don't know who you are or where you belong.
Prostate: A small gland that sits below the bladder near the rectum. It is part of the male reproductive system, and produces most of the fluid that makes up semen. When enlarged, it readily strangles the urethra, the passage through which urine and semen leave the body. Fluids, being similar to water, are associated with emotions.

Your sense of self, purpose and identity are connected in some way to something that has been cut off, restricted or constrained.
Your sexual performance has diminished; your manhood is challenged.
You reached retirement age and had to leave work, but you were not ready to go.

You were told you have reached your use-by date, yet you feel in the prime of life.
Your creative expression is being stifled and constrained, so you will have to find another outlet.
You are no longer free to express yourself.
You contained your emotions, and didn't show them.
Your sense of purpose has been taken away from you.
Your identity was connected to what you did for a living.
Your sense of self comes from what you do, not who you are.


## Sigmoid Colon problems

The main function of the sigmoid colon is to store waste matter until it is expelled from the body. If this process is delayed, other problems occur.

While residue is moving through the descending colon fluid is still being absorbed back into the body. Once the waste matter reaches the sigmoid colon, the absorption process should be completed. A problem with the descending colon suggests that in a given situation there is still something to be achieved. Whereas an issue with the sigmoid colon is saying there is nothing more to be taken from the situation, nothing more to give, nothing left to be of benefit.


## Urinary Incontinence

Urinary incontinence is the term for leaking urine. This can be caused by an overactive bladder, one that doesn't close properly, a blockage in the urethra or a physical inability and slow movement.

Losing control in other areas of life.
Slowing down and needing to hand over control.
Releasing what is no longer of use in an inappropriate way.
No control in letting go of something that must leave.
Not able to close something off.


## Urinary tract infections (UTIs)

Infections are caused by disease causing agents. In the lower urinary tract they are bladder infections or cystitis. In in the upper urinary tract they are called kidney infections.

The majority of UTIs are caused by E.coli bacteria that are commonly found in the lower intestines, most of which are harmless.

Harmful bacteria indicate that an enemy is present and it is connected to a group of like-minded people, where it finds strength in numbers. Someone could be strongly resistant to something or it could also be issues related to someone who has been around for a very long time.

The bladder is a temporary storage place for something ready to leave. A problem could show here when something that was meant to be a temporary measure has become a permanent one.

The urethra is a means of exit. An infection at this point could indicate that someone has invaded your space/life and won't leave. The exit is obvious, but they won't take it.

UTIs in females can be caused through sexual activity when the normal bacteria is displaced and relocated into the urethra. In such a case, the UTI could be associated with being displaced.

## Base Chakra and the foot

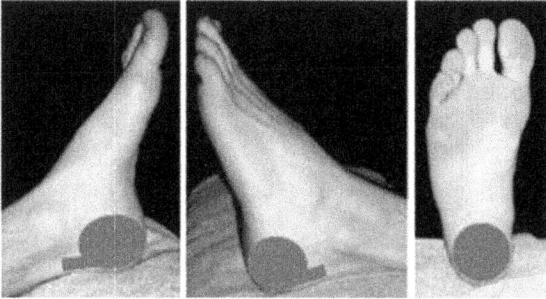

Position: plantar, lateral and medial heel.
Pain and discomfort in this area of the foot are related in some way to the family, tribe, group, religion or culture.

## Blisters
Blisters are caused by pressure from an outside source. Blisters on the heel could suggest that you are being pressured in some way by the group, family, tribe, society, tradition, religion or culture, or the pressure is related to some issue associated with them.

## Cracks
Cracks split the heels. Cracks to the heel could suggest splitting, separating or moving away from group, family, tribe, society, tradition, religion or culture.

## Callouses
Callouses are a form of protection. They consist of tough thickened skin as a result of repeated friction, pressure or irritation. They can be painful when pressure is applied directly to them. Callouses in the heel could suggest some form of protection related to direct pressure from the group, family, tribe, society, tradition, religion or culture.

## Plantar fasciitis

The plantar fascia is the band of connective tissue which runs along the sole, from the heel to the ball of the foot. From another perspective, the fascia runs between what the group wants (base chakra) and your personal rules and boundaries (solar plexus chakra), passing over the power games area of the foot (sacral chakra).

Any pain in this area could be caused by divided loyalties or a sense of being pulled in two directions. There could be a pull between what the group, family, culture or another wants, and what you want for yourself. Discomfort could also be related to how much you have to compromise your personal beliefs to fit into the group or maintain a relationship.

Who are you loyal to: yourself or others?
Do you find it difficult to find a balance between your needs and the needs of others?
Are you overshadowed by what another wants?
Do you do for others at the expense of yourself?
Do you feel as though you are in a tug-of-war, being pulled in two directions by others, your job or family dynamics?

## Plantar warts

Plantar warts are benign epithelial tumours generally caused by certain types of the human papillomavirus (HPV). They occur under the toes or on the sole of the foot. The virus attacks weakened skin, finding access through cuts and scratches. They are described as self-limiting as they are able to control their own growth.

Plantar warts, unlike ordinary warts, are sensitive to pressure, but more specifically, indirect pressure. They tend to be painful when pressure is applied from either side. Appearing in this part of the foot, you have to think about whether anyone from the group, family, culture, religion or tribe is applying pressure in ways that are subtle, indirect, hinted at, implied or merely suggested.

A general term for a virus, not specific to a wart, is a small infectious agent that replicates only inside the living cells of other organisms. This particular virus is spread by contact with an infected host, possibly in communal change rooms or shower floors.

Viruses are invasive. They invade your personal space and your body cells. So, is there anyone who has pushed their way into your life, and you can't seem to get rid of them? Is there someone who invades your space without being invited? Do you have a few tiny cracks in your armour, your vulnerable points, which someone has discovered?

A self-limiting organism or colony of organisms limits its own growth. Does a person with a plantar wart or warts limit their own growth by their own actions or non-actions? Do they know when too much or too many become self-destructive?

Anything that affects the skin is related to the integumentary system.

## Spurs

A heel spur is a bony growth under the calcaneus bone. When plantar fasciitis resists healing, the body attempts to repair the injury to the fascia with bone instead of tissue. Spurs are commonly found in joints and also where muscle, ligaments or tendons attach to the bone.

Strengthening your position within the group.
The group may be growing stronger as you pull away.
A radical way to heal a rift in the group.
Standing up for or supporting someone in the group.
Restructuring doesn't necessarily have to be painful.

## Seed corns

Corns form when the pressure point against the skin traces a circular or oval path during the rubbing motion. When such action goes round and round, it can indicate a sense of having no end, no way out, or no let up.

In this area, corns could indicate pressure from the group that never seems to end.

For more information, see Heart Chakra and the foot.

## Sacral Chakra and the body

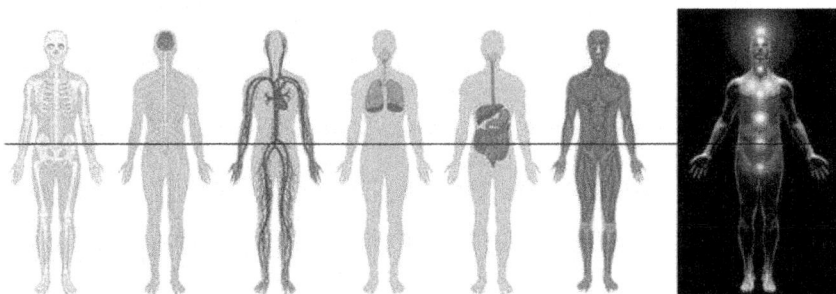

Areas of the body: sacrum, hips, gonads, lower back.
Pain, symptoms and disease that present in these areas of the body are related in some way to relationships, power games and material security including money and finances.


## Appendicitis

The appendix is a closed pouch, connected to the cecum near the ileocecal valve. It doesn't usually cause any problems until it becomes inflamed.

When the appendix is acutely inflamed, there is an urgency attached to addressing the problem as it could rupture. Often this requires surgical intervention. Appendicitis could indicate a situation which needs urgent attention before it explodes and becomes a much bigger problem. Outside help may be required to settle the circumstances. The appendix and appendicitis could be likened to:

A dead end street, going nowhere, with no exit point; you may have to retrace your steps.

A *No Through Road* sign. If you miss the sign, it might be a bit tricky trying to turn around and change direction, especially if your load is large and cumbersome.

A cul-de-sac where you have space to manoeuvre but you still have to come out the same way you went in.

Being backed into a corner with nowhere to go.

Being up against a brick wall with no way out.

A need to clear out what is working against you, and take a different approach.
A need to initiate a change, and begin to repair the situation.

When you are up against a brick wall, and the situation is urgent, and you have to make a decision, you always have a choice. You can blast your way through, or retrace your steps and go another way.


## Colon cancer
Cancer: You have lost your sense of identity. You don't know who you are or where you belong.
Colon: The place residue moves through before it is released.

Your sense of self and identity is somehow related to:
Something that you did in the past that has run its course.
Something that needs to move on.
Something that you need to let go of.
Something that is of no further use.
Holding on to something in the past as it validates and justifies your current position.


## Crohn's disease
Crohn's disease is a chronic inflammatory disorder in which the body's immune system attacks the digestive tract, possibly directed at antigens. It is also classified as an autoimmune disorder. The most commonly affected area is where the small and large intestine meet at the ileocecal valve.

*Valve* in the anatomy sense is described as *a flap-like structure that controls the one-way passage of fluid through an organ.*
Valves and sphincters are to maintain a one-way flow.
In comparison, a person has gone through a door that has closed. It is not meant to be re-opened.

When the valve leaks backwards into the small intestine, it could indicate that a person keeps revisiting some past event, is living in the past, or doesn't want to move forward with life. The comfort of the known could be more inviting than the challenges of the unknown.

Relates to finding an appropriate response in relation to:
Living in the past.
Moving forward as there is no going back.
Closing off from what has past.

95

Bringing closure to something.
Dwelling on someone/something that needs to be let go.
Resolving a particular issue.

When antigens and antibodies become involved, consideration must be given to a specific enemy. The antibody never forgets. So, whenever the same enemy (antigen) reappears, a specific defence procedure (antibody) is ready to attack.

Similarly a person may never forget their enemy, or what someone has done to them. They may revisit how they feel about it, over and over again, and always be on the defensive.

## Diverticulitis

Diverticulitis is a common disease of the colon where small pockets of the inner lining become inflamed or infected. The low-fibre Western diet is one of the most likely causes of this disease.

Little hidden pockets of discomfort or discontent.
Hiding something away that disturbs you, when it would be better to let it go.

This problem brings up questions like:
Why do some people continue to eat foods that are not compatible with their bodies?
Why do food choices only become important when a health issue appears?
Do you make food choices from habit?
Do you comfort eat?
Are you too exhausted by what you have to do (work) that you don't have the energy to do what you might like to do (prepare good food)?

The unsuitable foods you eat could pose the questions:
What else do you do that you know isn't for your highest good?
What other bad habits need changing?
What disturbs you that food comforts?

## Endometriosis

Endometriosis is the result of the tissue which lines the womb (endometrium) growing in other places, especially on the ovaries, bowels or bladder, resulting in inflammation and scarring. It is known to cause infertility.

When the endometrium tries to take over the surrounding area, it could indicate the desire and preparation to have a child could be taking over everything else in life.

When the endometrium causes infertility, it could indicate that there is an unacknowledged reason not to have a child.

An immature lining could indicate a feeling of not being ready for parenthood.

Scars and memories from childhood could be bringing up old challenges.


## Infertility

Infertility is the inability to reproduce by natural means. Common causes of female infertility include blocked fallopian tubes, ovulation problems or unsuitable quality of the endometrium. Male infertility can be caused by a low sperm count.

Blocking creativity.

Difficulty with self-expression.

Life is structured and ordered with set patterns; how well will you cope with the change?

Life will become unpredictable; you could lose control.

Everything has to be perfect and in place before you have a child.

Finances could become stretched.

Addressing the changing roles of parenting.

There may not be time for romance as you will be too tired.

Not sure of the future and what it holds.


## Irritable bowel syndrome (IBS)

IBS is a group of gastrointestinal disorders. Symptoms include abdominal pain and bloating, as well as frequent diarrhoea and constipation.

The cause is said to be unknown, but it may be triggered by stress, an infection, or changes in routine and diet. There is no known cure, and treatment is focused on improving the symptoms.

Unable to adjust to changes.

Needing to change your input into a given situation.

Changing how things are done for no apparent reason.

Adjusting routines and patterns.

Something could be blown up out of proportion.

Not giving a process time to complete properly.

Something/someone in your life isn't going to go away, so you will have to limit the effect they are having on you.

Managing an unpleasant situation to the best of your ability.

Someone on the team is causing harm in some way.

## Lower back muscular pain

A strain is the result of a stretch or tear to a muscle or tendon. Skeletal muscles can only pull in one direction. Therefore, they have to work in pairs. Each muscle group needs to work together to create movement. Fatigued muscles can be a forerunner to strains if the muscle group is overworked. Fatigued muscles need to be rested.

Are you pushing yourself to the extremes?

Muscle groups can also become damaged if not warmed up sufficiently before exerting them.

Do you understand *due diligence*?

Do you gather the facts and prepare before you begin?

Not knowing which way to go.
Lack of cooperation.
Unable to work with someone.
Needing help to do something.
Rejecting help.
Habitual and repetitive actions.
Pressure and expectation of others.
Being pushed around.
Being overworked, exhausted, fatigued and needing a rest.
Cramped and unable to move freely.
Being pulled in two directions.
Divided loyalties.

## Menopause

Some women can have a difficult time during menopause. If they don't take Hormone Replacement Therapy (HRT) they have extremely uncomfortable symptoms. If they do take HRT, they have a period. They are stuck. Whichever way they turn, they can't seem to win.

By the age of menopause, most women know what isn't working and what needs to change. Whether they are able to follow through and make those changes is another thing. That is when the body comes to deliver its message: change your life or suffer the consequences.

Menopausal symptoms are a result of hormonal imbalance, which draws attention to how you deal with authority figures.

The master gland in the body doesn't produce all the hormones required; it encourages the relevant gland to produce their own. If you have spent your life 'doing for others', menopause is the time to encourage them to do it for themselves rather than you continue to do it for them. It is time to explore your creative abilities, and discover what you are really capable of achieving.

If you have listened to criticism over the years, change what you have heard to constructive comments, and use this newly discovered information to your advantage.

If you have menopausal symptoms, a change in some area your life would be a good place to begin.

Some women need a little pharmaceutical help to begin with, but that doesn't mean it will last for the rest of their lives.

As you change your life, become your own voice of authority, and express your own unique creativity, you might be surprised how this impacts on other areas of your life and health.


## Ovarian cancer

Cancer: You have lost your sense of identity. You don't know who you are or where you belong.

Ovaries: Creative potential, expressing or not expressing creativity, shutting down and not developing potential.

Your sense of self and identity is somehow related to:

Continually putting yourself last.

Taking on the problems and needs of others as if they were your own.

Allowing the needs of family/others to determine and dominate your choices.

Shutting down your potential to nurture others.

Not following your dreams because you haven't found a way to incorporate them into everything else you have to do.

Fear of expressing yourself.


## Sciatica

Sciatica is pain in the buttock and leg, caused by pressure on nerves in the lower back. The sciatic nerve begins in the lower back, runs through the buttock and down the lower limb. The nervous system draws attention to the importance of communicating how you feel.

Aggression of some description that you need to talk about.

The need to address any power games that someone is playing; or, are you the one playing the power games?

Wanting changes within a relationship but are not able to talk about it.

Your ability to say what you think, or do you say what another wants to hear.

Avoiding difficult subjects and hoping they will go away.

Expressing your needs as others can't read your mind.

Do you hear the intended message or misunderstand what is being said?
Interpreting a situation through your own filters and bias.
Being worried about money or material security.
Something is challenging your financial security.
Being less than honest regarding financial matters.

## Sacral Chakra and the foot

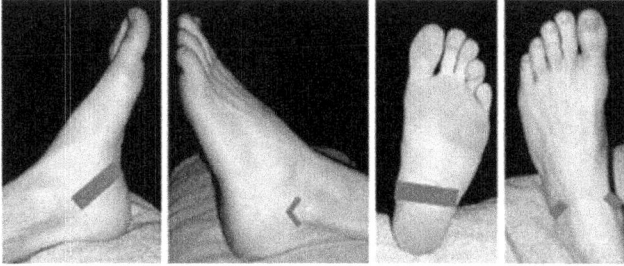

Position: ankles, lower soft plantar arch.
Pain and discomfort in this area of the foot are related in some way to relationships, power games and material security, including money and finances.

### Fractured ankle
When a bone is broken, splintered or fragmented, the message is related to something that has broken down, and needs to be restructured or rebuilt.

The ankle is the reflex for the hips, and is associated with restructuring a relationship or finance, and can include dealing with difficult people, power-games, money worries and material security.

### Plantar fasciitis
The plantar fascia is the band of connective tissue which runs along the sole, from the heel to the ball of the foot. It also stops the over-flattening of the arch of the foot which results in pronation or flat feet.

Pronation infers a person is in need of more support.

For more information, see Base Chakra and the foot.

### Sprained ankle
A sprain is a stretch or tear to a ligament. A ligament connects bone to bone, thereby supporting the joint and giving it movement.

A sprain can be the result of a direct injury, or when the joint is taken beyond its functional range of motion and limitation.

Being pushed beyond your comfortable range of motion.
A relationship that is tearing someone apart.
Stretching the friendship.
Taking finances to the limit.


## Swollen ankles
Edema (oedema) is the swelling of body tissue due to a build-up of fluid. The leaked fluid is called lymph. Immobility is a common cause.

The lymphatic system is constantly picking up what another part of the body has discarded as waste. It is responsible for cleaning up debris such as dead cells, and keeping the body clear of waste.

Therefore, people who are continually picking up after others, or want others to continually pick up after them, could find a problem with lymph and edema.

Fluid regularly leaks into tissue spaces. Therefore, edema may be related in some way to boundaries: ineffective boundaries, not respecting boundaries, someone is invading yours, or you are invading those of another.

When picking up after others never seems to come to an end, it can become despairing, especially when you are picking up negative emotions.

# Solar Plexus Chakra and the body

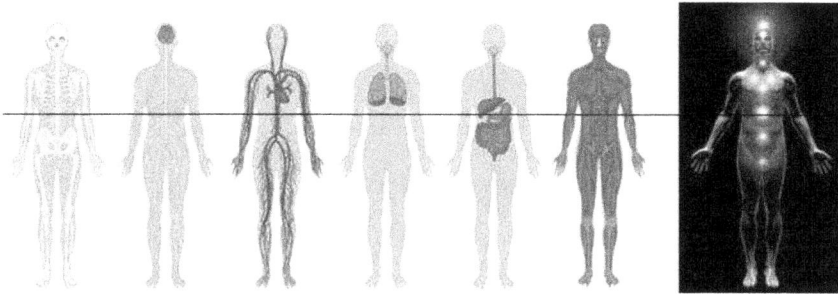

Areas of the body: lumbar spine, stomach, small intestine, pancreas, liver, gallbladder, lower thoracic spine, kidneys, adrenals.

Pain, symptoms and disease that present in these areas of the body are related in some way to the relationship with yourself, which includes your own boundaries and rules, and those of others.

## Celiac disease

Celiac disease is the inability to digest gluten, a protein found in wheat, rye and barley. It occurs because of an abnormal immune response which causes damage to the lining of the small intestines, and prevents nutrients from being absorbed. It is classified as an autoimmune disorder.

In Western society wheat would be classified as a staple food: something eaten regularly which forms a large part of the diet. Staple foods keep well over long periods and are available at all times. Having a reliable food source gives stability to a society or culture. Therefore, it is relatively easy to parallel a staple food such as wheat with a stable or unstable lifestyle.

*People are born with a genetic predisposition to develop celiac disease. Environmental factors play an important role in triggering celiac disease in infancy, childhood or later in life.*[6]

As it is described as genetic and affected by environmental factors, it is possible that unstable family patterns could also contribute. From a higher

---

[6] http://www.celiac.org.au/celiac-disease/#Celiac1

103

perspective, there is no criticism offered to the family as the child is the one who made the choice as to where they would place themselves.

Autoimmune relates to finding an appropriate response in relation to
An unstable lifestyle.
Constant ongoing adjustments.
A family who continually moves, not allowing someone to process the changes before moving on again.
An unstable family member.
A family member repeatedly displaying erratic behaviour.
A breakdown in a once stable family structure.
Divorce or death.
Multiple changes to the family structure.
Attacking or blaming an inappropriate person for something.

## Gallstones
*Gall*: something bitter or disagreeable, or something that causes vexation or annoyance; impudence, rancour, irritation and exasperation. Also meaning a sore on the skin caused by chafing or rubbing.

*Bladder*: a membranous sac usually containing gas or liquid.

Therefore, the gallbladder is associated with holding onto something bitter or disagreeable that causes vexation or annoyance. Issues with this organ could be directing your attention to something that exasperates and irritates you. Also something or someone could be rubbing you up the wrong way and causing you to erupt.

*Bile* relates to irritability or peevishness.
The main purpose of the gallbladder is to store and concentrate bile, a substance produced by the liver to help with the digestion of fats. It helps to emulsify fats and water, two liquids which are normally incompatible. Bile helps to combine these liquids, so that they can work effectively as one.
Problems connected to bile are related to getting on with incompatible people, those who you have nothing in common with, or don't particularly like.
Gallstones are small stones made from cholesterol, bile pigment and calcium salt, and are often said to run in the family. If thought contributes to what appears in life, could a strongly held family belief about a particular illness in the family line be self-perpetuating?
Therefore, gallbladder problems could be drawing attention to a relationship or connection that is completely incompatible with you, by dissolving any protective barriers and allowing a little freedom to move.

## Hiatus hernia

A hernia is caused by an organ pushing through an opening or tear in a muscle or tissue that would normally contain it. The upper stomach may break into the chest area because of a weakness in the diaphragm to create a hiatus hernia.

Something/someone has expanded due to a weakness of another.
Something/someone is in a place it's not meant to be.
Taking advantage of a weak spot.
Small windows of opportunity to expand.
Boundaries are being broken down.
Intruding on another or being intruded upon.


## Kidney failure

Kidney function includes regulating water, electrolytes and acid-base balance, and clearing nitrogenous wastes. Kidney failure occurs when the kidneys can no longer function properly, and can no longer remove waste products from the blood. Treatment for chronic kidney disease includes dialysis and kidney transplant.

Having to make difficult decisions.
Reaching a person's use-by date.
Feeling you have nothing more to offer.
Cannot accept inevitable change.
Cannot accept that it is time to leave a particular situation.
Resisting re-cycling something e.g. a particular skill.

It is not uncommon for people who reach retirement age to have kidney or prostate problems. There could be a feeling of reaching their personal use-by date and being of no further use. People who take a redundancy and cannot find similar work may need to consider other skills and areas of work.

Kidneys remind you to constantly monitor your life, be aware of what is going on around you, be prepared to make difficult decisions, and accept endings that may be unexpected or inevitable.


## Liver cancer

Cancer: You have lost your sense of identity. You don't know who you are or where you belong.
Liver: Accessory organ of the digestive system with many functions

Any process in the digestive system depends on the previous one being done properly. When someone isn't doing their job properly, it can make extra work for someone else.

If someone is carrying another person, whether it is in the workforce, a sporting team, as a carer or simply another family member, and they are suppressing their feelings for one reason or another, the liver could be the organ that brings attention to the underlying issue. While they are being responsible and doing what needs to be done, they could also be hiding their anger and resentment, sometimes even from themselves.

Functions of the liver include:
Production of bile which breaks down fats:
  Needing protection or having to have everything in its right place.
Detoxing the body of alcohol, drugs and poisons:
  Holding on to thoughts and patterns that don't serve your best interests.
Converting carbohydrates into glucose for energy, and storing the excess as glycogen until needed:
  Having too much of something, and holding on to it, just in case.
Converting ammonia to urea which can be excreted in the urine:
  Allowing transformation.
Removing and destroying bacteria and old red blood cells:
  Knowing when a cycle has ended and the ability to make difficult decisions.
Regeneration and re-growth:
  Knowing that when you are cut back, you can re-grow and renew yourself.

Cancer: Your sense of self, purpose and identity is associated in some way with the team.
Being part of an effective team.
Doing more than your fair share to keep the team running efficiently.
Hiding resentment for those team members who don't pull their weight.
Patience with a process.
Not expressing appropriate anger.
Working within structures; having a correct place for everything.
Staying the same and rejecting change.
A need to reassess your place in the team.

**Pancreatic cancer**
Cancer: You have lost your sense of identity. You don't know who you are or where you belong.
Pancreas: Its role in the endocrine system is to produce hormones, such as insulin. Its role in the digestive system is to produce digestive enzymes to help with digestion and absorption of nutrients.

Your sense of self, purpose and identity are connected to:
Authority and control issues (endocrine).
Being part of the team where everyone pulls their weight (digestive).
Being able to effectively put into practice what you have learnt or absorbed.
Being productive.
The ability to finish something off without outside help.
Producing something which benefits others.
Being of worth is connected to what you produce.
Results are more important than effort.
A sense of being controlled by someone/something outside of yourself.


## Reflux and Heartburn

Food passes from the mouth through the esophagus into the stomach. A sphincter (one way gate) stops the food returning. When the sphincter doesn't close properly, and food leaks backwards, the result is called reflux. Occasional reflux causes heartburn. Chronic reflux is known as GERD (Gastroesophageal Reflux Disease). Stomach acids can also escape and damage the lining of the esophagus.

Retracing your steps.
Moving forward and not going backwards.
Ending something off properly so you can move forward.
Not wanting to swallow something; some things are unacceptable.
What does your heart burn for?
What sets your heart on fire?

There are several sphincters in the alimentary canal, so the digestive system has a strong link to moving forward not backwards. Dysfunction in this system can also be a reminder to apply what has been learnt in a given situation, and keep moving on to the next stage of development.


## Stomach cancer

Cancer: You have lost your sense of identity. You don't know who you are or where you belong.
Stomach: Food moves from the mouth, through the esophagus, to the stomach. There it is broken down by stomach acid, and churned into a substance known as chyme. It continues on to the small intestine where it is further digested and absorbed.

Your sense of self, purpose and identity are associated with
The need to work with problems larger than they need to be.

The ability to break things down into workable pieces.
Living with, or avoiding the chaos necessary to improve a situation.


## Stomach ulcers
Ulcers are wounds or open sores that will not heal or keep returning. This simple description brings to mind an obvious underlying cause: a wound that won't heal, and is somehow connected to a team process.


## Type 1 Diabetes
Insulin producing cells of the pancreas are damaged or destroyed, resulting in high levels of glucose in the blood, rather than the glucose being absorbed and used by the cells.

As an autoimmune disorder it relates to finding an appropriate response in relation to:
Putting into practice what the person knows or has learnt.
Ignoring what the person knows or has learnt.
Absorbing what will be of personal benefit.
Personal growth through life's lessons and experiences.
Using energy to its best advantage.
Wasting energy.
Transforming hard work into tangible results.
Results and outcome overriding effort and contribution.
Authority and control issues.

Also associated with:
How well you take direction.
Needing to control people in your environment.
Feeling that you are the one who has lost control.
Feeling that you are constantly being criticised.

Type 1 diabetics can have a tendency to be subjective and take things personally, as against being objective, standing back and considering all options.


## Type 2 Diabetes
This disease is associated with lifestyle issues such as high blood pressure, poor food choices, overweight, obesity and insufficient physical activity.
Over a period of time insulin becomes increasingly ineffective at managing blood glucose levels, resulting in the pancreas having to work

harder, eventually damaging the insulin producing cells. The problem has been well established before a person becomes aware of it.

This disease could be associated with people who:
Feel they are becoming increasingly ineffective.
Have to work harder to achieve results.
Have suspicions about something, but do nothing, hoping the situation will go away.
Give up on something because it's too hard to achieve.
Repeatedly makes poor choices about other things in life.
Use food to fulfil an emotional need.
Ignore what is known to be helpful and beneficial.

Exercise, no matter how little, will be beneficial in some way, but there are many reasons why people find it difficult to do even a little, such as painful knees, sore feet, swollen legs, and shortness of breath. Every form of pain and discomfort is either a message or an excuse. It may be necessary to look at the hidden meaning of what is preventing the exercise before exercise can begin.

## Solar Plexus Chakra and the foot

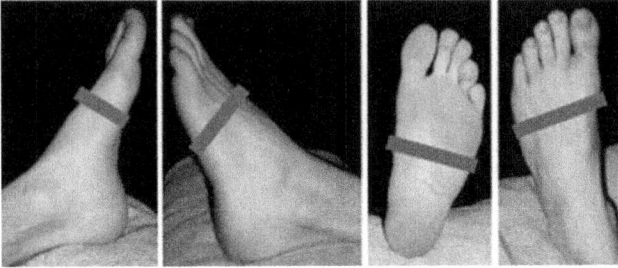

Position: upper soft plantar arch.
Pain and discomfort in this area of the foot are in some way related to the relationship with yourself, which includes your own boundaries and rules, and those of others.

### Fallen arches
Pronation and flat feet:
> Looking for greater support; needing to have more ground underneath.
> Wanting to connect with something strong and secure to feel safe.
> Needing the physical around you for security.

Limited connection of the toes to the ground could indicate these people are more grounded and practical than intellectual.
Finding security through physical or material surroundings.

### High arches
Supination and added lateral support.
> Needing extra support to find balance.
> Taking the long way to get somewhere.
> What is being avoided?

The heel connection with the ground implies stability, but the heavy connection of the toes to the ground could indicate these people spend a lot of time in their head.
Their thinking directs their lives.
Finding security through mind and beliefs.

# Heart Chakra and the body

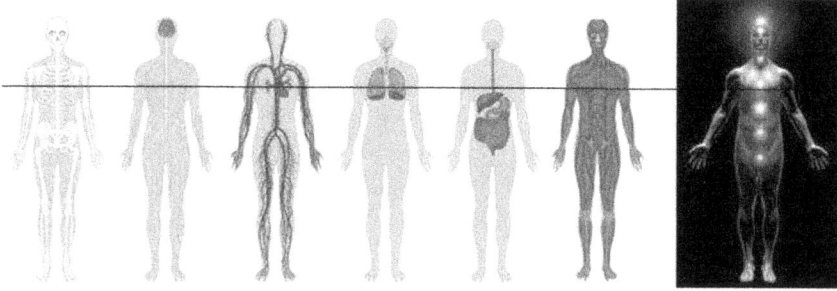

Areas of the body: thoracic spine, heart, diaphragm line, lungs, breast.
Pain, symptoms and disease that present in these areas of the body are related in some way to flows and blockages, being on the right track and persistence.


## Aorta aneurysm

An abnormal swelling or bulge in the wall of a blood vessel. They are most common in the aorta or blood vessels of the brain, and can cause death if they rupture.

An aneurysm in the heart area is related to action and the things you do:
Moving into dangerous territory.
Potentially harmful situations.
No respect for own safety.
Stretching boundaries to extremes.


## Asthma

Asthma is an inflammatory disease of the airways which can cause wheezing, coughing and shortness of breath, making it difficult to breathe in oxygen-rich air, our life-force.

Being cut off from a life force.
Someone or something you love and cherish has either left or changed.
Grieving for something lost or something that will never be.

Your life force is close by but difficult to connect to.
A sense of being squashed, crushed or suffocated.
A difficult transition or adjusting to change.
Someone closes you down and represses you.
Discipline that stifles your freedom of expression.
Overtaken by a sense of guilt, as you try to live up to expectations of others.


## Blood pressure

High blood pressure (hypertension) is increased pressure inside the arteries as it carries blood from the heart to the rest of the body.

The many ways a person puts themselves under pressure.
Pressure to stay on a particular pathway.
Exerted effort to keep doing something.


## Breast cancer

Cancer: You have lost your sense of identity. You don't know who you are or where you belong.
Breast: Nurturing, family, safety, needs being met.

Your sense of self, purpose and identity is related to nurturing others
Finding a balance between caring for the family and other pursuits.
Over-nurturing family/others at the expense of your own needs.
Under-nurturing yourself because others appear to have greater needs.


## Bronchitis (COPD - Chronic Obstructive Pulmonary Disease)

Chronic bronchitis is an inflammatory condition that causes the respiratory passages to become swollen and irritated. The symptoms include chronic cough, shortness of breath and increased mucous production.

Inflammation is part of the immune system, and appears when a perceived enemy is present.
Chronic inflammation can be an over-reaction to a perceived threat or enemy.
What do you need to get off your chest?
Overly protective of yourself or something/someone you value.

## Cardiovascular disease (CVD)
CVD is a group of diseases that involve the heart or blood vessels.

The cardiac muscle relates to:
Giving your all or not giving your all.
Persistence till the end.
Giving up.
Blood vessels are related to:
Being on the best path.
Following a path that someone else has laid out.
Avoiding what needs to be faced up to.
Existing through life, rather than living with passion.


## Cystic fibrosis
Symptoms usually begin in the lungs, with thicker than normal mucous that is difficult to get rid of. It is described as an inherited disease that affects the entire body. Family patterns, behaviours and beliefs that are passed from generation to generation are also part of the environment which can contribute to this health issue being described as heredity.

Someone or some belief that is overly protective and exclusive.
Something overwhelming that is difficult to dispel or escape from.


## Emphysema (COPD - Chronic Obstructive Pulmonary Disease)
Emphysema weakens the inner walls of the small air sacs in the lungs, which eventually break down, leaving a large air space instead of many small ones. This reduces the amount of oxygen that will be carried in the bloodstream. Smoking is the most common cause, but can also be the result of passive smoking.

Has anything collapsed and is no longer effective?
What could be in your environment that unknowingly affects you?
What is on the other side of your smokescreen?


## Fractured ribs
Ribs protect the vulnerable organs of the lungs, liver and heart, and most of the kidneys. When they are fractured, something has broken down, and needs to be restructured, rebuilt or supported.

Showing vulnerability.
Breaking down protective barriers.

Security dissolving.
Feeling exposed.
Needing to be less defensive.


## Heart attack and hardening of the arteries
Coronary artery disease, usually described as the hardening of the arteries, is caused by a build-up of plaque within the arteries, making them narrow, stiff and irregular, resulting in limited blood supply to the heart, which can cause

Myocardial infarction, commonly called a heart attack.
Angina, as blood supply to the heart is temporarily blocked.
The need for heart by-pass surgery.

Blocking passion and energy for living.
Making life more challenging than it has to be.
Inability to flow freely through life.
Being stuck in a rut or on a rigid life path.
By passing something that is too difficult to deal with.
Going around an issue rather than addressing it.


## Heart failure and cardiomyopathy
Heart failure develops over many years if the heart is unable to maintain a strong enough blood flow to meet the everyday needs of the body.
Cardiomyopathy occurs when the heart muscle becomes thickened, enlarged or stiff, reducing its efficiency. The two conditions commonly occur together.

I don't want to do this anymore.
Not wanting to meet the needs of another.
Counting the cost of what you do for others.
Conditional and unconditional love.
Not able to do what you once could do.
Feeling that a person's life is ineffective.
Becoming hard-hearted.
Needing more, but needs not being met.


## Lung cancer
Cancer: You have lost your sense of identity. You don't know who you are or where you belong.

Lungs: Enable you to breathe in oxygen from the air, and breathe out the waste product, carbon dioxide. The red blood cells deliver the oxygen and collect the waste. The cycle takes in and gives out.

Emotions: Grief, I should have been given more; guilt, I should have given more.

My sense of self, purpose and identity is connected to give and take, change and transition.

You don't deal very well with change.

Your identity and purpose are set.

You depended on someone or something which is no longer available.

You are in transition and not sure how you will manage it.

Your ability to give and receive is out of balance.

You find it easier to give than receive.

You believe that you are undeserving.

People may be taking from you, rather than you giving to them.

Your sense of identity was connected to a person who is no longer with you.

Your sense of identity and purpose is connected to what someone else wants.

## Heart Chakra and the foot

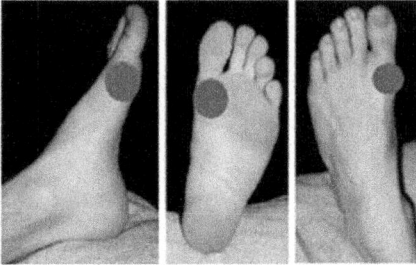

Position: ball of foot, bunion joint.
Pain and discomfort in this area of the foot are related in some way to flows and blockages, being on the right track and persistence.

### Ball of foot
A plantar wart in this area could suggest that someone is applying indirect or subtle pressure resulting in feelings of guilt.

For more information on plantar warts, see Base Chakra and the foot.

### Bunion
Bone issues around this area of the foot can be an indication of a stoic response: the ability or need to continue, no matter what the cost. It can suggest coldness and hardness, the loss of softness and ability to be pliable. This combination can also be related to shutting things out, or keeping them in.

The heart isn't necessarily about romantic love. It is more about compassion, commitment and giving unconditionally. There are many combinations that can result from bone and heart.

The heart, in relation to the cardiovascular system, is the pump that never gives up, and only stops at death. It works for the good of the rest of the body. The heart, in this context, can be related to unconditional love, not giving up, trusting that you are on track, counting or not counting the cost of loving others and what you do for them. These areas of life may need to be

116

restructured; your infrastructure (the inner strength) may have broken down and failed, or there could be a general feeling of a lack of support.

The emotions of the heart, in relation to Traditional Chinese Medicine (TCM), are joy, lack of enthusiasm and vitality, mental restlessness, depression, insomnia and despair. In TCM, joy refers to a state of agitation or over-excitement, rather than elation. The heart, in this context, can be related to the stoic response of existing, rather than living with enthusiasm and vitality, or the stoic response needed to stave off despair. Mental restlessness about something you believe you have to do for someone.

The issues of the heart, in relation to chakra energy, are concerned with compassion, gratitude, love, hate, forgiveness, intuitive knowing and self-nurturing. The heart in this context could be associated with a need to reassess your ability to be compassionate and grateful, to listen to and respond to your intuitive knowing, or consider a different perspective on love, hate or forgiveness.

Bunions relate to:

> The need to restructure your commitment to something or someone.
> An invitation to take more notice of, and act upon your intuition.
> The way your body deals with contained emotions in relation to unconditional giving or commitments.
> Your stoic response when you don't feel you have a choice.
> Inner strength failing.


## Gout
Gout is a type of inflammatory arthritis caused by a build-up of uric acid in the bloodstream, which crystalises and settles in a joint causing pain and swelling. The most affected joint in the body is the metatarsal-phalangeal joint (bunion joint). Joints are connective tissue in the skeletal system and are related to how a person connects with another, and possibly with the need to change.

*Crystallise*: To take on a definite or recognisable form, or give expression to. Also meaning to coat with sugar.

> Gout could be drawing attention to:
> A sugar-coated connection with someone.
> The need to define or give expression to something.
> An inflammatory relationship.
> Rigid, painful and debilitating connection to another.
> Icy cold, freezing another out.

## Seed Corns

Corns form when the pressure point against the skin traces a circular or oval path during the rubbing motion. When such action goes round and round, it can indicate a sense of having no end, no way out, or no let up.

Seed corns are clusters of small corns on the soles of the feet or palms of the hand. They usually show up within a callous, and can be very painful when pressure is applied, such as walking or gripping something. Friction and pressure contribute to their formation. Friction and pressure from shoes or holding on to something is only an indication of friction and pressure from someone/something else in another area of life.

A callous is a form of defence, and is the result of some type of friction over a long period of time. Blocked sweat ducts and dry skin are thought to be other causes of seed corns, which also appear on the plantar heel.

Friction and pressure that never seem to let up.
Not able to find a way out of friction and pressure.
Friction and pressure coming from many directions at once.
Trying to defend yourself from friction or pressure.

# Throat Chakra and the body

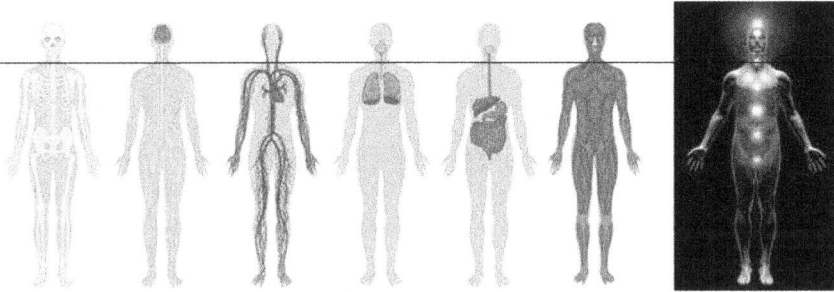

Areas of the body: cervical spine referring to the shoulder, including axillary nodes, throat, thyroid, neck, tonsils.

Pain, symptoms and disease that present in this area of the body are related in some way to taking responsibility, shouldering loads that aren't yours to carry, speaking up and flexibility.

## Dislocated shoulder

The humerus bone separates from the scapula bone at the shoulder joint.

Disconnecting from something/someone without causing any structural damage.
A connection/relationship needs repair.

## Frozen shoulder

The shoulder joint becomes inflamed and stiff, causing severe pain and limited movement. While the inflammatory response is part of body defence, it can also become part of the problem if the body doesn't monitor its response closely.

Frozen shoulder is associated with connective tissue and inflammation.
Connective tissue holds us together. How are you connected to others? Too tightly, and needing to break free?

Inflammation is part of body defence. Do you know how much is enough, and when to stop so that you do not cause further damage?

When something is frozen it becomes locked into a given shape.
Do you feel frozen in time or space; observing without being able to take part?
Have you lost the freedom to flow?
Wanting to reach out to someone and not being able to.
Giving too much and needing to reassess your movements.


## Fused vertebrae

Spinal fusion is surgery to the vertebrae or bones of the spine to connect two or more in such a way as to limit their movement and contain any pain caused by the joint. This operation is performed on other areas of the spine.

Not open to options.
Only willing to see one point of view.
Focused forward.
Not willing to divert from the pathway.
Direct communication is important.


## Goitre

A goitre is an enlarged thyroid gland which is usually associated with low iodine levels. It shows up as a swelling around the front lower neck and voice box.

The thyroid gland regulates metabolism and growth, and produces hormones. When the pituitary gland senses that the thyroid hormone is low, it sends a signal to the thyroid, but the thyroid can't produce the hormone without adequate supplies of iodine. Both an over-active or under-active thyroid can produce a goitre because of the overstimulation from the pituitary gland.

Working with inadequate resources.
Trying to make something from nothing.
Being pushed to achieve something.
Someone higher up the chain misinterpreting the situation.
Trying to achieve the impossible because an authority figure has directed it.
Wearing yourself out.

## Grave's disease

Hyperthyroidism, over-production of thyroid hormones, results in the metabolism quickening up.

The autoimmune response is related to finding an appropriate response in relation to:
Working too hard, pushing yourself, with little or no rest.


## Hashimoto's Disease

Hypothyroidism, underproduction of thyroid hormones, results in the metabolism slowing down.

The autoimmune response is related to finding an appropriate response in relation to:
Reducing work output, and giving yourself permission to slow down.


## Jaw problems

TMJ disorder is a general term for pain and dysfunction in the temporomandibular joint that connects the temporal bone in the skull with the mandible bone in the lower jaw and the associated muscles. Problems with this joint can limit movement and cause noise as the jaw moves. It is one of the more complex joints in the body.

Keeping your mouth shut.
Not speaking up.
Chewing over something that is causing pain and discomfort.
Your movements are limited.
Can't extend as you would like to.
Making an effort but not achieving much.


## Lymphoma

Lymphoma is cancer of the lymphatic system including the nodes.
Cancer: You have lost your sense of identity. You don't know who you are or where you belong.
Lymph: Tissue fluid that has leaked from the cells and collected by the lymphatic system becomes known as lymph. Once filtered, it can re-enter the blood as plasma.
Lymph nodes: Filter foreign material and cancer cells from lymph. They are part of the immune system and found throughout the body, including the armpits, groin and stomach.

The lymphatic system is associated with picking up debris and taking it away for disposal or cleaning.

Your sense of self, purpose and identity is connected to:
Continually picking up after others.
Absorbing what another has discarded.
Fixing someone else's problem.
Dumping or being dumped on.
Squeezing through boundaries.
Being on call and always available.

## Mouth ulcer

A mouth ulcer is usually the result of biting the tongue or cheek, or a cut from a sharp tooth.

Bite your tongue.
What would be better left unsaid?
Regretting something that was spoken.
Some sharp edges need smoothing off.
An open wound.
Indicating something relatively harmless that will heal itself.

## Rotator cuff

A rotator cuff tear occurs in the tendons that hold the rotator cuff muscles in place.

Something that is holding you together is being torn apart.
The load you carry is too heavy to sustain.
Shouldering responsibilities for others.

## Sore throat

As part of the respiratory system, the pharynx filters, warms and moistens air, and provides a passageway into the lungs. As part of the digestive system, it assists in swallowing, and provides a passageway for food to reach the esophagus.

Most sore throats are caused by a virus, a disease carrying agent which can only reproduce in the cells of a living host. Once attached, viruses reproduce quickly.
Virus: something that needs a host to latch on to as they are powerless on their own.

Some sore throats are caused by bacteria. Strep throat is an infection at the back of the throat caused by bacteria.

Bacteria: something that can cause harm in their own right as they do not need anything from you to help them grow and spread.

Allergies can also cause sore or itchy throats.

Allergy: being close to something that you are incompatible with, or over-reacting to something or someone.

Air and food share this narrow passageway. They have to cooperate. Therefore, throat issues caused by a virus, bacteria or allergy could be related to:

Having to share a confined space with someone else.

How well you function when under pressure.

Having to get on with someone who irritates you.

Working closely with a domineering person.

Giving someone the space they need to perform properly.

What is stuck in the throat that you can't speak about?

Someone is invading your space.

Something/someone could be taking over and using you in some way (virus).

Something/someone is spreading out without your help (bacteria).

## Stiff neck

The cervical spine is made up of seven vertebrae and several types of joints, and is the most mobile area of the spine. A stiff neck can be the result of constantly looking backwards, over your shoulder, and covering your back. Whiplash can be when you are whipped back to have another look at something.

A stiff and painful joint in the neck can relate to:

Being rigid, structured, inflexible, unbending, formal or fixed in relation to your speech and how you address others.

Being rigid, structured, inflexible, unbending, formal or fixed in relation to the responsibility and loads you carry that don't belong to you.

Being too flexible, ready to change direction at any given moment.

Being forced outside a comfortable range of movement.

Who is being a pain in the neck?

## Tonsillitis

Tonsils defend against disease carrying agents trying to enter the body through the mouth or nose. They filter foreign bodies, and block entry to potentially harmful agents.

Infected tonsils are most prevalent in children. From a child's perspective:
Something is or is about to be forced down their throat.
Something that is completely foreign to them is being pushed down their throat.
Something is about to enter that could be harmful.

Besides food and physical objects, rules, beliefs, family patterns, acceptable behaviour and how everything should be done could be some things foreign to the nature of the child, that are being blocked from entry.

Tonsillitis is also common in adults even when the tonsils have been removed.
What is making you angry or inflamed?
What potentially harmful force could you be trying to stop from entering?

## Throat Chakra and the foot

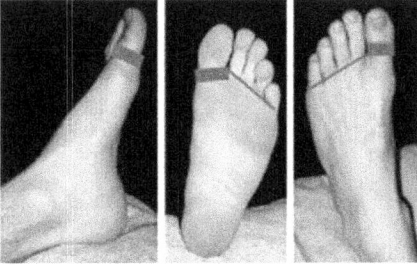

Position: base of hallux, extending across the base of all toes
Pain and discomfort in this area of the foot are related in some way to taking responsibility, shouldering loads that aren't yours to carry, speaking up and flexibility.

## Tinea

Tinea is the umbrella name for a group of highly contagious fungal infections of the skin. It is called Athlete's foot when it appears on the feet. While these infections are not serious, they can cause itching and irritation between the toes. Tinea is easily picked up from wet floors in public areas if not wearing foot protection, or by sharing an affected towel.

There are many different types of fungi in our environment, but only a few, in comparison, make people sick.

Something or someone has spread out very quickly.
The need for you to spread quickly.
Taking due care around certain conditions.
Being irritated.
Boundaries erupting.

## Painful webs of toes

Webs of the toes are one of the shoulder reflexes in the body. When they are painful, it could indicate carrying responsibilities that aren't yours to carry.

When the tendons on the upper foot pull the toes towards the body, it indicates shouldering heavy loads, sometimes from an early age, when a person may not be ready to carry them.

The base of the big toe and the adjacent web reflects the neck. Pain in this area indicates a problem with the neck, or whiplash.

Constantly looking over your shoulder.
Covering your back.
A quick look back at something.

# Third Eye Chakra and the body

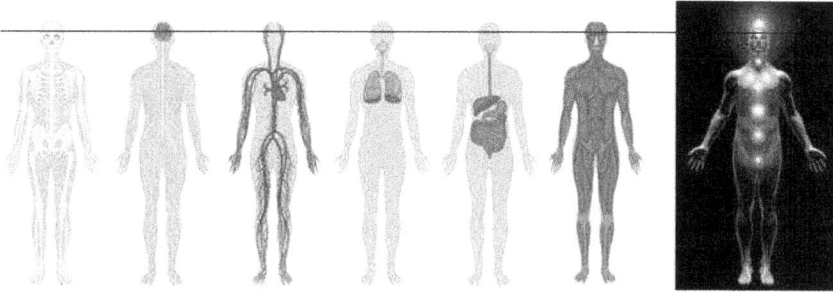

Areas of the body: nose, sinuses, eyes, ears, pineal, pituitary and hypothalamus glands.

Pain, symptoms and disease that present in these areas of the body are related in some way to closing the mind, making something right or wrong, being open to the paranormal and unexplained, or being overly logical and analytical.


## Dry eyes syndrome

Dry eyes are described as decreased tear production or increased evaporation. A decreased tear production could infer that a person is holding in their emotions and not expressing them: not allowing their feelings to flow.

As evaporation occurs from the surface of a liquid, dry eyes could relate to a superficial level of dealing with something that is causing grief, expressing insincere emotions, or not being prepared to delve too deeply into the situation at hand.

Dry eyes could also infer that a person has run out of tears, cried too much, no energy left or exhausted.


## Headache (frontal)

Frontal headaches that cause pain across the forehead are mostly related to sinusitis, eyestrain and tension, but can also include the brain freeze ice-cream headache.

These headaches could be indicative of someone whose opinions are 'black and white' with no ability to compromise or accept that there can be 'grey' areas in life that lack definition.

Making something/someone right or wrong.
Judgments.
Being pulled in two directions.
Putting yourself under tension.
Not able to relax and accept life as it is.
Closed mind.
Not prepared to see options.
Frozen thoughts.


## Hearing loss

Age-related hearing loss could be nothing more than not wanting to hear something. If you have been listening to the same old, same old thing for years on end, maybe you just don't want to hear it any more.

In speaking to someone who is profoundly deaf, a person needs to be face-to-face, and slow their speech a little. This could be related to taking the time and effort necessary to understand what someone is trying to say. It could be about connecting with someone when you are speaking to them, rather than just throw them a few words in passing. The profoundly deaf could be helping to clear family patterns in past generations.

Like many disabilities that people are born with, the person concerned has made a choice to have this experience. Without the profoundly deaf, some of the wonders of medical science would never have been developed. Society owes them a debt of gratitude.


## Insomnia

Insomnia is physically related to the pineal gland, which produces melatonin, a hormone that affects a person's waking and sleep patterns. If this gland isn't producing the appropriate hormones at the appropriate times, the body becomes confused about when it needs to be awake and when it needs to sleep.

Insomnia is related to being spiritually awake or asleep, walking in the light or being stuck in darkness, and a mind that is open or closed.

The pineal gland helps you to differentiate daytime from night, and is connected to enlightenment and dispelling the darkness.

Symbolically this is the place where the mind takes control through thoughts and logic. Insomnia could be asking you to consider a higher meaning to life and apply it to the physical reality in which you live.

When the person is awake at night, what are they thinking about?
Judging someone or something to be good or bad, right or wrong.
Refusing to see from another perspective.
Closing their mind to certain areas of their life.
Not being able to see past the physical result of something.
Allowing logic to run their life.
Dismissing possibility or anything that is not understood.
Inability to see that life is exactly how it is meant to be.
A hectic and busy lifestyle (reassessing priorities and expectations).
Not enough time.
Seeking approval from another.

As we open to enlightenment on a metaphysical level (third eye chakra) our bodies will adjust to a cycle of light and darkness on a physical level (pineal gland) and hopefully we will sleep peacefully in trust, knowing all is well (without insomnia).


## Macular degeneration
The macula is the small central portion of the retina which is the light sensing nerve tissue at the back of the eye. Deterioration causes loss of central vision which means many every-day activities become difficult.

Messages delivered by macular degeneration are not simply about distorted sight, but vision in general.

Unable to see what everyone else can see.
Interpreting reality in a different way to others.
Unable to see the big picture.
Unable to identify the ramifications of a given choice.
Unable to clearly recognise what is in front of them.
Warped perception.


## Meniere's disease
Meniere's disease is a disorder of the inner ear that usually affects hearing and balance. Symptoms can include vertigo, tinnitus and hearing loss, ranging from mild to severe.

Inner ear labyrinth: I'm running around in circles. I can't find a way out. My life is out of balance. It might be much better if I couldn't hear anything.
Vertigo: I'm trying to stand still, but everything around me is in constant motion. I'm being drawn into it. I'm losing control.
Tinnitus: I don't want to hear a certain sound/voice, so I'll drown it out with a louder one of my own.

Meniere's disease could be related to a primary caregiver who is on call every day, and never seems to have a moment to themselves or any time off: someone such as a busy mother of young children, an adult child of aging and frail parents, or a dedicated volunteer who helps the sick, disabled or less fortunate.

Their needs, calls and voices are constantly being heard, over those of the caregiver.

## Sinusitis

Sinuses are hollow cavities found in the front of the skull, including the forehead, cheeks, the top of the nose and behind the eyes. They have several purposes, one being a resonance chamber for speech. When something resounds, it goes round and round and round.

What thoughts are going round and round and round in your head with no outlet, no expression and no end in sight?

What issues are you always coming face-to-face with that need to be closely monitored and subsequently addressed?

Sinusitis is an indication that inflammation is present. Inflammation is part of the immune response to eliminate the cause of the infection, and begin the repair process.

The presence of any infectious agent is an indication that something has invaded your space without invitation. As with any immune response, the body needs to monitor it closely. Too little inflammation may be ineffective to the healing process. Too much inflammation can compromise the cells and lead to other problems.

Sinusitis relates to closely monitoring what you are doing in certain situations. Too little involvement may be ineffective. Too much may cause long-term damage.

## Tinnitus

Tinnitus is a noise or ringing in the ear/s, which is a symptom of a hearing problem. While the most common cause is exposure to loud noises, softer sounds and certain frequencies can also cause the problem.

The noise in your ears could be connected to another voice/noise that you are constantly hearing:

A crying baby, fighting children, frail and elderly parents.

What noises and sounds do you not want to hear?

What do you need to shut out?

Silence and quiet time are something you may crave.

Are you the one person everyone comes to when they need something?

As tinnitus is only heard by the person experiencing the symptom, are they the only one that needy people continually call out to?

Are you trying to drown out the guilty voice that is always telling you what is your responsibility and what you should be doing?

## Vertigo

Vertigo is a sense of dizziness; a feeling of spinning round in circles or swaying back and forth when the person is standing or sitting still, or a feeling that everything around them is moving when it are not. Vertigo is aggravated by moving the head.

You are trying to stand still, but everything around you is in constant motion.
You are being drawn into something without your consent.
There is too much going on.
You feel you are losing control and going round in circles.
Do you need to stay extremely still and not move?
Do you want to say, *Leave me alone*?
You are fixed and refused to be swayed.

## Third Eye Chakra and the foot

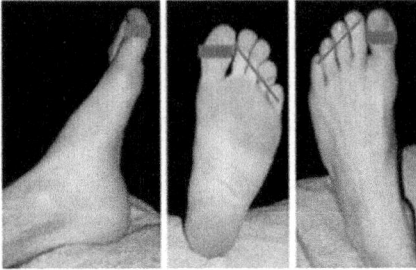

Position: base of the nail of the hallux, extending across all toes.
Pain and discomfort in this area of the foot are related in some way to closing the mind, making something right or wrong, opening to the paranormal and unexplained, or being overly logical and analytical.

## Arthritis

Arthritis is a general term for inflammation of the joints, and often appears in the toes and fingers. The joint is unable to function properly due to pain, swelling and stiffness. Osteoarthritis is a degenerative joint disease where cartilage and bone breakdown in the joint, due to wear, tear, age or trauma. Rheumatoid arthritis is an autoimmune disorder.

Arthritis in this part of the foot could be connected to:

Something breaking down or wearing out.

Mental processes slowing down or not functioning properly.

Painful connections.

Appropriate responses.

Self-critical thoughts, attacking yourself.

## Paronychia

A paronychia is an infection to the tissue at the base or side of the nail where it meets the skin. A relatively minor injury can become infected by fungi or bacteria, causing redness, pain and swelling.

Nails are an appendage to the integumentary system which is related to the first line of body defence and temperature. Skin also contains receptors that respond to stimuli. Nails protect the nerve endings in the fingers and toes and allow for greater sensory input.

Therefore, it relates to:

Your ability to recognise and respond to stimuli.

Not responding as expected.

Sensitivity blocked, insensitivity.

Protectiveness.

Being inflamed or angry about what you or someone else is thinking.

## Crown Chakra and the body

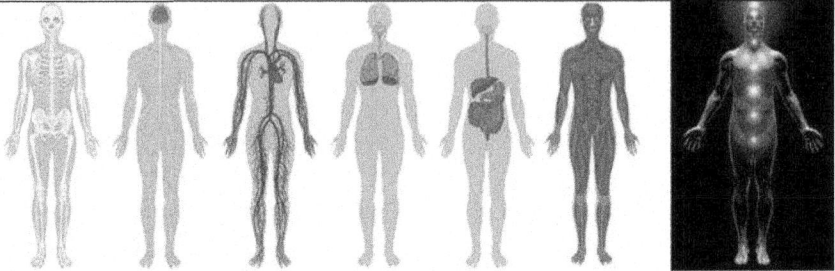

Areas of the body: Brain, skull, hair.
Pain, symptoms and disease that present in these areas of the body are related in some way to trust and vulnerability, letting go of control and ego, connecting to Spirit, self-mastery and transformation.

### Brain aneurysm

An aneurysm is an abnormal swelling or bulge in the wall of a blood vessel. They are most common in the aorta or blood vessels of the brain, and can cause death if they rupture. An aneurysm in the brain is connected to control and communication.

You could move into dangerous territory if you communicate what you really want.
A potentially harmful situation could arise if you say what you think.
Speaking up could risk your safety.
Explosive communications.
Stretching boundaries to the extremes through communication.

### Brain tumour

Tumour: You have lost your sense of identity. You don't know who you are or where you belong.
Brain: The communication and control centre. It takes in all forms of data, interprets the meaning and formulates a response.

Your sense of self, purpose and identity is connected to your ability to communicate accurately who you are and what you want, and be in control of your own life, without being misinterpreted. For some reason you can't be your authentic self.

Who is controlling your life?
Someone or something else is trying to take over.
Needing to communicate to your higher self.
Your spiritual beliefs are intrinsic to who you are, but people don't want to hear about them.
Identity crisis.
Needing to change your environment.

## Cerebral palsy

Cerebral palsy is a disability that affects movement and posture. Messages from the brain are misinterpreted which affect muscle response, resulting in uncontrolled movement. Communication pathways are affected, not the muscles themselves.

Cerebral palsy is usually the result of changes in, or injury to, the developing brain before or during birth, or sometimes in early childhood.[7] The precise nature of the injury is not known.

By choosing to enter this lifetime with a disability, a person may be fine-tuning something they need to experience, to balance something from another time or help to dismantle long established family beliefs about something. In this case, the person may have agreed to teach lessons related to either or both of the body systems involved.

What can cerebral palsy teach others about communication and control?
Everyone communicates in a different way.
It's easy to misinterpret messages.
Some inappropriate responses are unintentional.
People may not be able to control a situation, no matter how hard they try.
Reaching potential is different for everyone.
Overprotectiveness may not be a suitable response.

What can cerebral palsy teach others about divided loyalties?
Do people do things they should do, rather than what they want to do?
Does guilt play any role in decision-making?
What motivates people?

---

[7] https://www.cerebralpalsy.org.au

Someone is over-involved and doing too much.
It's okay to put yourself first.
Some lifetime commitments can be difficult.


## Dementia

Dementia is a collective term for a wide range of symptoms associated with a decline in memory or cognitive processes which severely reduce a person's ability to perform everyday activities. Alzheimer's disease is the leading form of dementia.

Remembering what to do and how to do it becomes difficult. Controlling everyday body functions and retaining communication skills are also a large part of the problem.

Information overload, can't keep up.
Too many choices.
Life is so complicated, it used to be simple.
Living in a world you don't understand any longer.
Life is moving too fast; once you were able to keep up.
Everyone's in a hurry; what happened to patience?
No one has time for you anymore, they're all too busy.
You have chosen to step out of the rat race, and slow the pace down.
You are not particularly interested in the present, the past is what brought you joy and happiness.
You don't like what the world is coming to, so you'll create your own.
You want to escape, but you are not ready to go for good just yet.


## Fractured skull

The skull offers protection to the brain. The brain is the control and communication centre.

Infrastructure has collapsed or is being challenged.
Finding a new way to protect a vulnerable part of you.
Needing a breakthrough in some form of communications.
A need to restructure spiritual beliefs.
A need to be open and talk about your spiritual beliefs.
Something may not be as strong as you thought it was.

## Head lice

Head lice and their eggs (known as nits) are parasitic insects mostly found on the head close to the scalp. They feed on blood, and can cause the scalp to become very itchy. They are most common in children.

A parasite is an organism that lives in or on another organism (host), and takes whatever it needs to grow.

An unbalanced relationship where one person benefits at the expense of the other.
One person is draining energy from another.
Boundary are being trodden on, and the host is reacting.

## Headaches (top of the head)

There are many causes for pain in this area of the head, including tension, symptoms of other diseases, lack of sleep, coughs, colds and nasal infections, or even pulling your hair tightly.

Pain around the crown could feel like the skull is too small and constricting: squeezing, squashing and crushing a person. The role of the skull is to protect the vulnerable brain: the control centre.

On a metaphysical level, it could be the doorway to your higher selves. Feeling pressure on this part of your body could be an indication of shutting out your potential and refusing to connect to all that you could become.

Headaches on the top of the head could be indicative of being stuck in an ego, which is only an image of who you are. They could be an invitation to let go of control, trust the unknown, and connect to the spiritual.

## Meningitis

Meningitis is an acute inflammation of the meninges, the protective membranes covering the brain and spinal cord. Bacteria meningitis is serious and needs urgent medical attention. Viral meningitis is more common but not as dangerous.

Whatever protects you is under threat.
Communication networks are being attacked.
Protective barriers are being destroyed, with or without your help.
Something relating to control and communication needs urgent attention.

## Multiple sclerosis (MS)

MS is a disease of the central nervous system where the insulating covers of the nerve cells are damaged.

Autoimmune diseases are related to finding an appropriate response.
Protective communications.
Damaged communications which need to be fixed.
Not saying what needs to be said.
Letting or not letting others know what you think.
Interpreting sensitivity and vulnerability as weakness or failure.
Insulating yourself inappropriately.
Feeling frail and fragile.


## Parkinson's disease

Parkinson's disease is a disorder of the central nervous system that mainly affects motor skills. It is the result of cells dying in the part of the brain associated with reward and movement.

Early symptoms include tremor, stiffness, slowing movements, stooping and shuffling. Sometimes categorised as a movement disorder, the symptoms gradually increase over time.

The cause is generally unknown, but believed to involve both genetic and environmental factors, and often affects members of the same family.

Rewards don't match effort.
Other areas of life where control is slowing slipping away.
Difficulty in responding the way you would like to.
Complexities of doing what you are being asked to do.
Ignoring something that is deteriorating.
Ineffective messages and communication.
Can't connect with others the way you used to.
Family patterns and beliefs about the disease.


## Spina bifida

Spina bifida is a condition that occurs when the vertebrae of the spinal column do not close completely around the developing nerves of the spinal cord, leaving the nerves exposed or damaged.

Insufficient folate or folic acid in the diet during pregnancy plays a significant role in this condition as it is important in aiding rapid cell division and growth of the embryo. It is also needed to make and repair DNA.

Something seems to be getting ahead of itself.
Starting a process without having all the essentials.
Communication processes are left wide open and could cause damage.
Damaging communication.
Restructuring or closing off communication.

## Stroke

Cerebrovascular disease is connected to blood flow to the brain. A stroke occurs when an artery supplying blood to the brain becomes blocked or bleeds, causing a blockage or a haemorrhage. In either case, brain cells die and part of the brain ceases to function properly.

Unable to communicate how you feel about life, love and passion.
Bottling something up until it eventually explodes and destroys the surroundings.
No longer in control of life, as every pathway seems to be blocked.
Trying to stay in control with limited resources.
Can't seem to get through to people anymore.
While losing control in some areas, you gain control in others.
Needing to face the reality that you can't do what you used to do.

## Crown Chakra and the foot

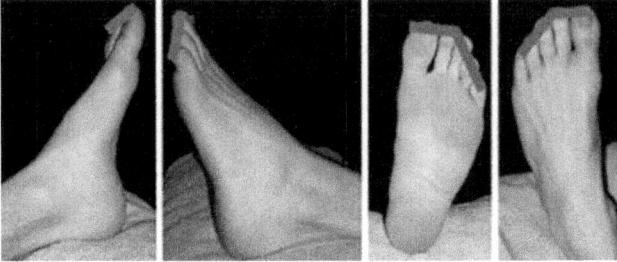

Position: top of the toes.
Pain and discomfort in this area of the foot are related in some way to trust and vulnerability, letting go of control and ego, connecting to Spirit, self-mastery and transformation.

## Curled toes

Toes that curl downward and under, and look like they are digging into the ground, could indicate:

Shutting down potential.
Stubbornly holding your position.
Closing down.
Fixed connections.
No flexibility.

## Ingrown toenails

Ingrown nails are described as the sides and corners of the nail curling down and growing into the skin. The most common cause is said to be tight-fitting shoes and cutting the nails low into the corners.
Nails are connected the liver, which holds the emotions of anger and resentment.

Something is growing inwards.
Being subjective or self-centred.
Anger focused inward.
Readily blaming something or someone.
Encouragement to look within for answers, even if it may be painful.

140

## The Worksheet

You may have already discovered the message that a particular disease, symptom, pain or sickness is trying to convey, but just in case you are having any difficulty, you might like to put all the pieces of the puzzle together using this worksheet.

If you don't know the answer to the questions about the physical body and ailment, you can always do an online search. Remember, you are only looking for the most basic explanation of what body systems do and the function of particular organs or body part. If you look too deeply for an explanation, you could easily become lost in detail.

You are also only looking for a starting point and a possibility. Once you find that, you may be surprised how quickly the rest of the puzzle comes together, and becomes clear to you.

What is the disease, symptom, pain or sickness you are trying to understand?
•

Where is it showing up in your body?
•

From a chakra perspective, what lifestyle issue resides in this area of the body?
•

What side of the body is it on?

- 

Who might it relate to?

- 

What body system is associated with this disease, symptom, pain or sickness?

- 

What is the basic function of this system?

- 

How do you connect this particular function with what is happening in the chakra area where the problem has presented?

- 

If an organ is involved what emotion could be suppressed?

-

What was going on in your life when the problem began?

●

# Part III

## Energy Shifts in Everyday Life

Some experiences as energy shifts can be quite unsettling. As the mind begins to lose control, and tries to understand what is happening, it can battle to regain its power. Fear is one of its most effective weapons, as it tries to convince you that something is wrong. It is as though part of it is dying, and in its death throes it will do whatever is necessary to regain its position of control.

As energy changes in the subtle body, the effects are felt in the physical one. As energy is blocked, the body experiences negative results such as illness. As energy is raised, vibrations change, and confuse the mind, who is ceaselessly trying to analyse, understand and explain what is happening. Therefore, positive energy shifts can take time for the body to adjust to, and feel comfortable with.

Many clients have experienced these energy changes as a feeling of cold. As vibrations change, the mind interprets them as shivering, and so convinces the person that they are cold. Blankets, heaters, warmer clothing or hot baths will not make a difference, because the feeling is not connected to temperature. As the body adjusts to this new vibration, and incorporates the changes, the feelings of coldness subside.

When someone feels freezing cold during an energy session, I am sure that some profound shift has taken place.

Not all energy shifts occur in a clinical situation, with a practitioner working in energy fields. Some occur at self-development workshops, but many occur in everyday life, and appear quite unexpectedly.

In understanding that chaos is an essential element of functioning at a higher level, sudden disruptive experiences can be understood in a different and positive light. Disorder and chaos can be the power necessary to break through what is no longer serving your highest good, and setting you on a pathway more appropriate for your particular time and place.

There are many minor energy shifts every day, some freeing, others blocking. But, then there are the major shifts, the ones that take time to process. It is as though in climbing the mountain, you have reached a plateau, where you will rest, process and apply what you have learnt. Then, eventually you will continue on your journey.

We all have our own chakra stories as energies realign, clear or balance. Some would be easily recognised as we consciously joined in the experience. Others may have become clearer in retrospect. Either way, they were transformational moments, for as your energy changes, your circumstances follow.

In sharing my seven chakra stories, I hope to remind you of your own, and the moments when blocked energy is freed, giving you a little more clarity of your purpose and potential, bringing with it a greater sense of harmony and balance.

# Held captive by hidden beliefs[8]

## Base Chakra

For many years I had absolutely no idea what I was doing here. As I grew in awareness, I realised that I had chosen to come, understood the role my family played, identified the limiting patterns and beliefs, and what I needed to do to reach my potential.

Clarity and awareness didn't necessarily bring with them a life free of difficult and unpleasant experiences. They did, however, bring an understanding that allowed me to process my circumstances and emotional responses quicker than I might have expected.

I put myself into a post-war family in 1947. My sister was fourteen months older than I was, and together with my mother and father, grandparents and unmarried auntie, lived together in the old family home until I was almost seven.

I had chosen a family with parents who would give me the opportunity to stay with what felt comfortable until I was ready to explore further, an older sister who would be a guiding light and a fountain of information once I set out on my own path of discovery, a grandmother who would instil in me beliefs that would carry me into adulthood, a grandfather who seemed somewhat isolated, and an auntie who was more like a second mother.

I was around fifty before I understood how beliefs and patterns sat in the subconscious, and controlled me by subliminal messages. It was also many

---

[8] Based on Lessons 1 and Lesson 4, Wisdom in Retrospect, Emma Gilbert, 2014
Here I am again; I must like this place
*I chose the circumstances of my birth, including my family, timing and lessons*
Absorbing information; adults always seemed to know what was best for me
*I learned behaviour patterns and beliefs as a child that I never knew existed*

years before I realised that I had a purpose for being here, and the best way to discover what it was, was to discover what it was not.

Religion and God turned out to be an important part of this journey, but more specifically, it has been about discovering God outside of religion. Maybe that was one of the reasons I chose a family who were good people with Christian values, but rarely, if ever, went to church.

Surprisingly, one of the first things my parents did was to send me to Sunday School at the Anglican church from the age of three, every week, without fail. At eighteen I became a Catholic, and by twenty-five, I was attending daily Mass and saying the fifteen decades of the Rosary most days. If my plan was to discover God on my own terms, it was going to take me another twenty-five years before I consciously got started.

In those years I gradually learnt what I didn't want in life, which was slowly defining what I wanted. While I distanced myself from the religious tribe at the age of fifty-four, I am grateful for the experience, because without it, I wouldn't be who I am today.

By this age, I knew that my life path was no longer connected to a religion, but I still wasn't sure what it was about.

About this time I discovered that the beliefs learnt in childhood could still be influencing the decisions I made, and ultimately controlling my life.

Once again, I looked back to the tribe, but this time it was the family tribe, and it was my grandmother, Clara, who stood out. As a child, I had perceived her to be the dominant female of the family.

In the past I would have blamed Clara for teaching me certain limiting beliefs, but now I would describe it more as: *she drew my attention to certain areas of my life that would need my focus as I grew older.*

What I learnt from her wasn't necessarily taught directly. I could have gleaned my information from the general conversation in the house as three generations all lived closely together. Either way, certain words and phrases were deeply embedded within my psyche which would dictate my responses and choices for the greater part of my life, without my knowing.

Clara taught me:
*Children should be seen and not heard.*
Not that I wasn't allowed to speak – I was – but there were many unspoken innuendoes attached to her comments that displayed control, and contained expectations of politeness and restraint.

So, if I was going to speak up, write books and present controversial ideas and concepts, I would have to address any resistance to expressing myself when what I said may not be readily accepted by others.

*Money doesn't grow on trees.*

I could well have learned a *lack mentality* through observing the financial situation of our family, and the general state of the world in those years. This was re-enforced by the fact that we couldn't afford our own home, and had to live with relatives for several years.

So, if I wanted to live in abundance, in any shape or form, I would eventually have to come to believe that I had the ability to create whatever it was that I wanted.

*A woman's place is in the home.*

The majority of women from my grandmother's and mother's era didn't join the work force. They stayed at home, and looked after the family. Home seemed to be the inevitable destination for a woman in those years. Even in my childhood, most girls left school aged around thirteen to fifteen.

If I was going to join the workforce, open my own business, and travel the world, and not feel guilty about what I was doing, I would seriously need to redefine the role of this particular woman.

In looking back to the tribes that I had aligned with – both family and religion – and considering what they had taught me, I was able to identify important reasons for being here. I could also recognise what I would need to address in my life if I was going to apply what I was learning, and to follow a particular pathway.

And while a person may walk away from the tribe, they can unknowingly take beliefs and patterns with them which can hide for many years, and reappear without warning.

# Someone took my seat

## Sacral Chakra

In moving away from the group, you take yourselves with you. If you haven't applied what you learnt from them, you take the same old patterns and issues and apply them to new relationships.

This is where a learning experience can turn into power games, if you don't understand that the other person is helping you to identify what needs to be addressed, and changed.

Residue from your survival days, outdated beliefs and behaviour patterns can sit in hiding, just waiting to be set off. For the greater part, you can think you have dealt with something, until, one day, your reaction to something surprises you.

Not all that long ago, I went on a day bus trip with three other people while on holiday. Mini buses picked everyone up from their hotels, and took them to a meeting point where we boarded a larger coach. Our mini bus was the last to arrive, meaning that the coach was almost full, with few seats to choose from.

Knowing the area well, I knew that the remaining seats were on the shady side of the bus both going and coming, which meant that I wouldn't have to sit in the sun all day. Happily, we all settled into our seats with expectation.

The first stop was about an hour later. Everyone got off the bus for coffee, food or a walk around. To my absolute surprise and amazement, when I got back on, two people had changed seats and were now sitting where my friend and I had been sitting. I was surprised at how angry this made me feel.

My friend and I moved further down the bus, but the air vent wasn't working which resulted in a gale force wind targeting her body. So, she moved over on to the sunny side. I didn't. I sat in my seat and stewed. I was furious that my seat had been taken. I was also amazed at my reaction.

I have never said that people shouldn't allow their feelings to well up and be expressed. I have always maintained that any sort of intense emotions are simply drawing focus to something that is unresolved and needs attention. When you don't understand that principle, you can wallow in negativity for some time and become very unhappy. But then, sometimes it takes a few minutes or hours to let the emotion settle enough to be able to think something through.

When we got off the bus at the next stop, I told my friends about how I was feeling, and in particular how surprised I was at my reaction to losing my seat. I was somewhat surprised at their reactions.

Firstly I was reminded that I didn't have a reserved seat on the bus and that anyone could sit anywhere. That was true, but what about the unspoken rule that said if a person chose their seats, then that was where they sat. My logic said that if I was on a week-long trip, then change around each day, but one day seemed different.

My idea about unspoken rules was quickly challenged. They may have been my unspoken rules, but they weren't necessarily those of other people. I took the point.

Then I was reminded that I didn't like keeping rules, so why should other people keep mine; mine being if you choose your seat, you stay there all day.

So the issues of the sacral chakra were beginning to come into play. Firstly because something unresolved from the past had surfaced, and secondly my emotions were still running a bit high to think about the situation from someone else's point of view. I didn't necessarily want my friends to agree with me, but I did want some sort of understanding which I didn't feel I got at that point.

How could I make myself feel better? Get my original seat back. So, when it was time to get back on the bus, I made sure I was first on, and that I sat in my original seat. I somehow felt justified, a lot calmer and ready to process the emotions and what they meant.

What had just happened? Old patterns that had ruled my life for many years had surfaced and tried to take control. Understanding how unresolved issues sit in waiting, makes it quicker to process something unpleasant and move on.

For many years, I kept all the rules. I was the good child, the attentive wife and the dedicated church-goer. Eventually I wouldn't conform to the rules of others any longer, and made my own.

So, in this situation, I am again experiencing someone making me do something, and giving me no choice. And again, I didn't speak up and say anything. I kept quiet and did as I was told.

This has been a pattern for most of my life. Doing something I didn't want to do to keep the peace.

And while I didn't say anything to the people concerned, I did something to change the situation. I sat in my original seat, which from my perspective was my way of standing up for myself.

I did wonder if I had gone and sat in the front seat behind the driver what those occupants might have said to me. I somehow thought they would have told me that I was sitting in their seats.

The other challenge that came to the fore was whether there actually are unspoken rules. By the end of the day I had decided there were; no other person on the bus changed seats.

So the challenge to myself and others was about unspoken rules: those that belonged to me, and those of society in general.

And whether anyone on the bus agreed with me or not, I allowed myself to make my own rules about bus seating and keep them. I gave myself permission to be angry and I allowed my friends to have their own perception of the whole event.

We had a lovely day together.

It may have seemed quite petty to have gotten so upset over a seat, but it wasn't about a seat. It was about an unresolved issue that I needed to have another look at. Power games will only erupt when you don't remember that you allowed another to start off a process about something that you need to deal with. In this case those people where complete strangers.

As you move into your solar plexus energy, you need to set your own boundaries, make your own rules, give yourself permission to be yourself, and honour who you are, whether others understand or not.

# What on earth was I thinking?[9]

## Solar Plexus Chakra

In deciding that the rules of the group were too restrictive, and the rules of a relationship could break down into power games, it was time to consider which would be the best rules for me to apply to this game called life.

I allowed my tribe and family to set the ground rules, until I was able to set them for myself.

If I paid attention, I would learn critical information about myself through another, which would help me reach my potential.

Now, as I enter into my solar plexus energy, it is time to define who I am and what I believe. In the process I will discover and respect the boundaries of others.

Self-definition requires boundaries, and personal boundaries come in many forms: your own rules, honouring your own needs, the necessity of being able to say *no*, and the ability to put yourself first.

And, these are the basis of this story.

Over the years I had come to the conclusion that everyone else's needs were more important than mine. If I had them, they were so well submerged, I wouldn't have recognised them.

Everyone seemed to come before me: my husband, my children, friends, the poor and needy, and the neighbours. Somehow, I felt responsible to make everyone's life more pleasant and comfortable.

My religious beliefs seriously encouraged me to give to those less fortunate. I seemed to do most things in the extreme. I swung between

---

[9] Based on Lesson 20, Wisdom in Retrospect, Emma Gilbert, 2014
What on earth was I thinking; how much was I supposed to be doing for others?
*My values needed to be re-assessed and my priorities changed*

martyrdom and victimhood on a regular basis. I had no understanding that I was invading the boundaries of others, and could be dismantling a self-created lesson, which would have to be set up again and again.

At that time I didn't know how to honour my own boundaries, so I had no idea about those of anyone else.

Then, one of my Good Samaritan acts got seriously out of hand. These days, I would describe it as my higher consciousness stepped in to give me a lesson in respecting boundaries, especially my own.

In the early 1990s we invited a woman on a methadone programme to come and stay with us for a few weeks. I had met her through my husband's involvement with the St Vincent de Paul society. It was Easter at the time, she was lonely, and my husband felt sorry for her, so I agreed to a short stay.

At the time she didn't mention a few vital details about herself and her friends, such as growing marijuana, police involvement and over-dosing on a blood thinning medication, which caused severe internal damage, hence her methadone programme for pain relief. Her medication was controlled because of her history, which meant I had to drive her to the chemist each day to receive the dose.

The first few days of her stay were okay, but then she began to drink. Her medication mixed with excess amounts of our alcohol which she drank throughout the night while we slept was not a good combination.

And so, my husband went off to a St Vincent de Paul conference in another city for the weekend, feeling confident that I could handle everything, as always. Early on the Saturday morning, I knew the situation was deteriorating and fast getting out of hand. She'd been up and down all night drinking, was now depressed and waving a knife, threatening to kill herself. My three young children were in the next room. I needed some help. I rang my husband, who didn't want to know about it, so I rang a friend, who came immediately.

Eventually an ambulance arrived, but wouldn't take the woman to hospital because she refused to go, and they couldn't use force. So, the police were called; for some reason two police cars were needed to keep the situation in hand.

In the middle of the trauma while she was threatening to cut her wrists, I thought I had better get the children – aged about nine, eight and three – out of the house. I took them next door to the neighbour's.

When the woman was finally taken off to hospital, I went to get my children. I was apologising to them for what had just happened, 'I hope you weren't too scared.'

'No,' answered my nine year old son, 'I see it on television.'

*God Almighty,* I thought, *what am I doing to these kids.* They didn't seem to know the difference between television and real life.

I discovered later that this woman had been searching through every drawer and cupboard in my home, and had taken many of my things. I found them hidden inside containers, which were inside other containers, which were hidden inside bigger containers and boxes. They were very well concealed in her own belongings which were in our garage.

That was just one of many similar stories that displayed how I vacillated between the martyr and the victim. I was so fixated on saving the world that I had no concept of invading the boundaries of another, let alone any thoughts of how to protect my own, and those of my children.

That experience was a huge learning curve. It brought boundaries to my attention with great urgency, but I wasn't quite ready to put myself first, not just yet.

I eventually learnt to put myself first, when I accepted the fact that I had a choice. The subtle and not so subtle programming from my childhood and religion had convinced me that to put myself first was selfish. I came to realise that putting myself first was essential. If I was healthy and happy, calm and contented, doing what I wanted to do, rather than all the things I should be doing, then everyone benefited.

The choice wasn't between specific entities, ideas or things. The choice was about the consequences of the decision, and which of those I would prefer to live with.

In later years, my clients re-enforced the concept of choice, over and over again. Many said they didn't have one, but I knew they did. As I saw people getting frailer, sicker and unhappier because they wouldn't choose in their own favour, I became more convinced that self-priority was essential.

The first time I consciously put myself first was when I went to Israel. I was working as a parish secretary at the time, and a group was making a pilgrimage. I had done a lot of work in putting the trip together, so I decided, rather than wave everyone goodbye, I would go with them.

Of course, this radical decision brought up many of my old beliefs and patterns, to challenge and keep me captive, but I was strong enough within myself, by this time, to put them aside, and continue along my path, misjudged by some as *selfish*.

I don't think anyone in my family actually believed that I would go, until I was almost on the plane.

I was learning to free up the energy of my solar plexus. I had set my own boundaries, and learnt to honour those of others. I had put myself first without feeling guilty. I acknowledged that I also had needs, and respected them.

# It wasn't my time to leave

## Heart Chakra

As we journey towards our heart chakra, we once again think about how we chose this lifetime and allowed the experiences, what we have learnt about ourselves through others, and the changes that followed which defined us as an individual, who respects and honours themselves.

As we come closer to the heart, we feel a calmness that defies understanding, a knowing that all is well, and a deep trust that our inner guidance will never lead us astray.

We will not leave this earth plane until we have finished what we came to do. Some will leave after a very short time, others will stay many, many years.

This is a story about perfect timing, trust, and knowing that I won't leave by mistake. When I eventually go, it will be on my terms.

My sister and I went to a concert in the city. A few of the golden oldies were getting together to sing some of their more famous songs. I drove, and we put the car into a parking station a little distance from the venue.

It was after 11pm when the concert finished. We walked back to the car to head for home, but the boom-gate at the parking station didn't want to open. I tried the ticket several times, but nothing was happening.

There were very few people around, so I wasn't quite sure what to do next. When in doubt, always talk to angels. Eventually the boom gate lifted, and we drove out.

The street we pulled into had a slight incline. It was about 800 metres to the top of the small hill where we would turn left. It was one-way with several cross streets. Considering it wasn't all that late at night, there was almost no traffic around.

155

I remember looking up this almost deserted street. There was one car in another lane on my right, but predominantly I remember the green lights at every corner all the way up. We would have been driving about 50 kph.

All of a sudden, from nowhere, in front of me, almost touching me, making a right angle with my car, was another car. My sister saw it at the same time.

I hit the brakes with force. We were only a few metres into an intersection.

The other car was flying, and obviously had driven through a red light.

That's when some strange things began to happen.

It was as though everything slowed down and I was watching a video in slow motion. I remember sitting tall and straight in the driver's seat, watching what seemed to be the two cars dancing and embracing each other.

The front left of my car and the rear of the other car seemed to be melting together and blending with each other somehow. All I could remember thinking, over and over was, *Anytime now, anytime now.* I was obviously waiting for the impact and the crash. But, nothing happened. I just kept watching these two cars dancing together; dancing was the best way I could explain it.

I have no idea how long this lasted but the next thing I remember was the other car parked in the centre of the road about 100 metres away to the left. It was an old style car, dark in colour and the occupants were looking back at us. They didn't get out. They drove off.

It was only then that I started to shake a bit. I remember saying to my sister that something very weird had just happened, and I had no idea what was going on.

My car hadn't stalled, and the engine was still running. As I began to drive off, I realised that I was in exactly the same place as I was when I first saw the other car in front of me. I was still in the same place where I had slammed on the brakes.

Later I checked stopping distances and found that a car travelling at 60 kph would take 56 metres to stop. My car was still in the exact same position, just a few metres into the intersection.

If the braking distances were correct, I should have skidded through the intersection, and been well on the other side.

My sister later said that she couldn't see the front of the bonnet from where she sat. That seemed to make sense as she was shorter than me, but when I sat in the front seat again, no matter how straight and tall I sat, I couldn't see the end of the front bonnet either.

There was a time when I would have said that I had no idea what happened, but now I would say that we stepped into another dimension, and maybe

156

while in that other dimension we had a choice as to whether we stayed or came back.

It obviously wasn't our time to go. The boom-gate at the parking station held us up long enough so that we wouldn't be in the middle of the intersection when the car sped through, which would have given my side of the car the full impact. The fact that the other car was going so fast also contributed to a safe ending.

This potential accident held a profound lesson for me, one that I may not have had to experience if I had trusted my intuition and followed my inner guidance. It was related to publishing one of my books, *Wisdom in Retrospect*.

I had become unnecessarily concerned about time and costs. I knew I would eventually inherit a small amount of money, and I was playing it safe and waiting. The universe was plainly telling me that I needed to get on with what I knew I needed to do, and let everything take care of itself.

The potential accident clearly showed me that I could die at any time, to presume nothing, and to act on my inner guidance, not just listen to it.

# Clearing the family line[10]

## Throat Chakra

If I am going to live on the earth until I accomplish what I came for, then I may as well do it consciously, and on my terms. I can only create a life of choice if I accept responsibility for everything that presents itself. If I have created it, then I can change it. If someone else created it, then I am powerless to make the change.

If, in my dying breath, I was asked about the most essential thing I had learnt in this life time, I would have to say: responsibility. I was responsible for all of it.

While I had thought about this concept for some time, it finally became crystal clear in Hawaii in 2006 at a Ho'oponopono conference.

I had known from past experiences that when I attended a conference or workshop it would take me to a higher level of awareness. My body always went through some sort of detox in preparation. I usually came down with a cold, the respiratory system being the easiest way for the body to detox. The body would let go of physical *stuff* taking the emotional *stuff* with it, ridding itself of old patterns and beliefs to make way for the new.

The experience in preparation for this conference wasn't going to be any ordinary detox cold like in the past; something huge was about to shift and it would need something huge as a lever.

---

[10] Based on Lesson 58, Wisdom in Retrospect, Emma Gilbert, 2014
Ho'oponopono, the ancient Hawaiian practice of reconciliation
*I am responsible; on some level of my consciousness I have allowed, created or drawn to myself everything in my life*

I returned from overseas a few months before the conference. A few health things were happening, but I wasn't connecting them to the conference in Hawaii, and the inevitable preparation I would be undertaking.

I was very dehydrated on my return, but didn't realise it. I also had a nose bleed, and didn't know that it was an indication of dehydration. I didn't take too much notice, except inside my nose still wasn't healing.

A few weeks later it rained and the *skin cancer weed* (euphorbia peplus) finally showed up in my garden. The dry weather had kept it from sprouting, while the sun spot on my nose waited patiently. I had used this weed several times to treat sun spots, and it always worked.

I was more than generous with its milky substance, and as usual, it blistered and went to a scab, but this time it didn't heal. It just kept slowly weeping. I thought I had used too much.

Inside my nose hadn't healed, and was becoming a problem. It reminded me of what my feet had looked like many years before when I had dermatitis: crusty weeping sores that wouldn't heal.

About the same time, cold and flu symptoms presented themselves. I woke up after a restless night with a very sore throat and swollen neck, as though I had tonsillitis, except they had been removed when I was young.

I still hadn't asked the obvious question, "What is this all about?"

I was sure it was somehow connected to the conference in Hawaii, so I left it at that.

A few days later as I looked in the mirror and noticed how red my nose was, like I had been badly sunburnt.

Within a few hours, it was twice its normal size. After a few more hours, my face was beginning to swell. It was hot, red and hard to touch. What if it spread into my eyes and I couldn't see, or further down into my throat and I couldn't breathe?

For the first time, my symptoms had my full attention. What were they trying to tell me?

The progression of events seemed to begin about the time I had registered for the conference. There had to be a connection. It had to be part of the multi-level detox my body was going through in preparation. I had expected something but not anything like this.

I stood in my bedroom and had a serious talk to my nose. It was time I knew what this was really all about.

Answers often come in concepts; something like a deeply complex explanation, appearing in flashes of intuitive knowing that are interconnected on many levels with your entire being: an explanation that you absolutely understand in an instant, but could never put into words and explain fully.

Recently, when I helped my mother move, I found a photo of my father's mother. It had been a long time since I had thought about her, so I placed the photo on display in my bedroom. As I looked at her young face, I could only remember a stooped old lady, with grey hair in a bun, who moved slowly.

As I looked at her photo, I realised that I couldn't remember her name. The name just wouldn't come. I couldn't believe that I didn't remember my own grandmother's name.

Was she so insignificant, that she had faded from life unnoticed, and unremembered, even by members of her own family?

Now, as I looked at her photo, I instinctively knew that she was involved somehow, and was helping me do something.

This quiet and unassuming woman, who seemed to pass through life, almost unnoticed, was helping me. If skin issues were the clue to what she was helping me with, then it had to be something about insignificance, being on show and stretching my boundaries.

My father's side of the family had always suffered with skin problems. Past generations had worked in hat factories and they all appeared to suffer with an allergy to felt and green dye. The skin problems had stayed in the family line even though nobody worked in hats anymore. My father was discharged from the army with skin problems. I had dermatitis which became septic as a teenager. Skin problems were in the family genes. They were believed to be hereditary.

As I looked for more clues, I thought about recent events, but more importantly took note of what words I had been using to describe them? I realised that many times during those few months I had thought, *everyone's stuff is in my face.*

My husband was a messy hoarder. His stuff was everywhere, inside and outside the house. I had just moved my mother and my auntie to new homes. I had to deal with their stuff for months, especially the stuff that needed to be thrown out, that they wouldn't let go of. My daughter had stored a lot of things at our house for many years and was about to move, so I had gathered all her stuff together, and left it in the lounge. It was just sitting there.

Everywhere I seemed to go I had someone else's stuff *in my face.* So if any issues were about to be processed, it was quite possible that it would show up in my face. The fact that the stuff belonged to everyone else could be the clue that it would be a collective issue of some kind, while the stuff belonged to them, also belonged to me.

The antibiotics I had taken for the previous few days had made almost no difference. My face was still hot, red and hard, and as I lay in bed early on that Saturday morning, I knew it was only a matter of hours before I would need to go to hospital.

Not that I thought for a moment I was going to die, but as I lay there my mind flashed to my father. He had died four months before he turned sixty. I was four months off turning sixty.

Bells rang and lights flashed. I knew that all my bodily discomforts over the past few months were related to clearing something in my father's family line that he wasn't able to do before he died.

What issues had been suppressed in the family line that surfaced as skin problems? Skin marks the physical outer boundary that contains us. It defines how we are recognised when we are on show. It is what people see when they look at us.

From a metaphysical comparison, skin problems can be messages related to being stretched, the need to expand and change, gathering courage to push through the boundaries that contain you, or allowing something that is sitting below the surface to erupt and make its presence known. It also brings attention to moving out of your comfort zone into the unknown, and being at ease when standing out and being on show.

As I looked once again at the photo of my grandmother, I knew that the skin issues in the family line had a lot to do with feelings of insignificance, lacking confidence, fear of self-expression, and a desire to stay in comfortable places.

The time of hiding away was coming to an end. My boundaries were about to be extended in ways I couldn't imagine. Before too long I would be putting myself and all my ideas on show, standing out and being acknowledged.

The beliefs that had held skin problems in my family line for many generations were being addressed. By understanding the messages of the body, I was able to identify what beliefs were not serving my highest purpose and dismantle them, bringing me a little closer to self-empowerment and reaching my potential.

I spent a few days in hospital on intravenous antibiotics. My face took several months before it lost its redness and was back to how it used to be.

Deep within I would never be the same. I had changed. I had cleared the way for something new to enter. I had done my preparation and was ready to go to the conference, and while this story is related to responsibility and the throat chakra, the problem showed up in the area of my third eye, inviting me to open my mind to the many unexplainable events that would follow.

# Meeting with the unexplainable[11]

## Third Eye Chakra

The throat energy helps you to understand that your hidden beliefs add an intrinsic contribution to what shows up in your life. The third eye energy invites you to consider other expressions of what is hidden and unseen. It invites you to the esoteric – with its psychic connection – challenging ideas, other dimensions and all things unexplainable or difficult to understand.

For many years I had set ideas, a closed mind, and thought I knew what life was about, when in fact, I didn't have a clue. I lived with tunnel vision, outside of a world that I didn't know even existed.

Going back to college to study reflexology took me to a new world with many challenging experiences. I was intelligent and logical, and thought that I could explain most things, but I was soon to learn differently.

For a long time I didn't tell this story to anyone who didn't know me well, as I thought they wouldn't believe me.

It is about psychic phenomena, the unexplainable, and other life forces, all of which challenged my logic and helped me to open my third eye.

After this experience, I knew I didn't have the answers to most things in life. I was very comfortable with having no idea about many more things.

I signed up to do some sort of personal development live-in week. I had almost no idea what it was about, but one of my clients had gone along, and I knew that at some time, I would go as well.

---

[11] Based on Lesson 46, Wisdom in Retrospect Emma Gilbert, 2014
I never took visiting other dimensions and meeting aliens seriously, until….
*There are some things that cannot be explained within the limits of the physical universe*

I thought I would take along a bottle alcohol and chocolates, just to top off a hard day's work if it turned out like that.

Little did I know that this was more than personal development! It was spiritual, mental, physical, and emotional stretching as I had never been stretched before in my life. There was fasting and cleansing, amongst other things.

I could have cheated and had a drink and some chocolates in the evening – nobody would have known as I was staying in a motel room on my own – but if I was going to play the game, I may as well give it my best shot. By the end of the week, I hadn't opened the alcohol nor eaten any chocolate.

So, on the way home, I decided to empty the whole bottle into the ocean, as part of a personal closing ritual of sorts.


The beach I went to was contained between two headlands, maybe two kilometres apart. I had parked my car at one end and, taking the bottle, walked to the water's edge. I began walking northwards. I could see two people in the distance, much further up the beach. It was a very secluded area.

I walked for about fifteen minutes along the edge of the water, stopped, opened the bottle, and tipped it into the ocean. I felt good. I wanted to mark this spot somehow, so I walked to the back of the beach, stood there for a moment and tried to do a *gorilla call*: the sort Tarzan did as he beat himself on the chest; the sort we had been doing on and off during the past week.

The first one didn't come out, so I tried again. I vaguely remember falling backwards as I heard my voice resounding out loud.

I fell backwards into soft white sand for what seemed like a few seconds. When I opened my eyes and looked around, I was puzzled. There were now about eight people on the beach further up from where I was and they couldn't have got there in a few seconds. It wasn't possible. I sat in the sand for a few moments with my jeans rolled up to just below my knees and the sleeves of my shirt rolled up to my elbows. If I felt good before, I felt amazing now.

I ran back to the water's edge and began jogging back to the car. I started flicking at my hair thinking, *I'll have to get all this sand out of my hair before I get back into the car.*

I had fallen very heavily, so I knew I would be covered in sand. I flicked my hair a second and a third time, and was surprised that not much sand seemed to be falling out.

As I had a two hour drive home, all I wanted to do was get the sand out of my clothes, off my feet and out of my hair before I got back into my car. As I neared the car park, I headed away from the water, looking around for a tap to wash my feet.

As I was washing them, I realised there was very little sand on them, only some on the soles where I had just wet them. I had walked on beaches many times and knew that if my feet were wet from the ocean, sand would stick to them and cover them.

I also needed to get the sand out of my clothes before I got into the car. I began rolling down my right trouser leg to shake it. Not a grain of sand was caught in my clothing. I am not exaggerating! When you fall backwards into soft white sand and lay there for what I later estimated to be up to thirty minutes, there must be some sand in your clothes, at least a small amount somewhere.

I rolled down my right shirt-sleeve, the same thing: not a grain of sand anywhere. I didn't check the left side of my clothing for any sand as I was sure it would be the same.

I was beginning to become a little spooked as I got into the car and began to drive home, but at the same time I felt so invigorated, rejuvenated and revitalised that I was able to put the unexplained aside for the moment.

The feelings of exultation soon changed to something close to horror. The drive home was one of the most frightening experiences I can remember. I never thought that I would arrive home safely. I was convinced I was going to have a major accident. I was sure I was going to die.

I was driving as I would usually drive on a busy highway and keeping to the speed limit. Cars, trucks and semi-trailers around me didn't seem to be driving at great speed but somehow I had a feeling of being left behind.

Something odd was happening that I didn't understand – something strange and frightening. It was as though I was physically in my car but actually somewhere else. I was confused and disorientated, but didn't connect how I was feeling with the experience on the beach a short while before.

As I arrived home, I noticed the time. The clock must be wrong.

I remember exactly what time I had left the motel because I sat in the car talking to someone, and the news had come on the radio. I knew how much conscious time I had spent on the beach. I knew how long it would take me to drive home, so I couldn't be home as yet. There was about an hour missing. I couldn't possibly have done what I did and be home in such a short space of time. I was beginning to become very confused.

Just then my son drove in. Only then did I roll down the left side of my jeans and my left sleeve. Like the right side of my clothing, no sand. No sand in my clothing combined with a journey that should have taken at least another hour. What was going on?

My mind was being asked to step outside of anything it could possibly explain.

What I hadn't initially known about the course that I had been on for the past week was that it had been held in an area that was in some sort of portal or vortex, an entry point to and from other dimensions for other life forms.

This was well outside of my logic and reasoning, and if I had known about it in advance, I may not have gone. But go, I did, and now it was over. As I sat in the comfort of my own lounge room, still somewhat confused and apprehensive, I began to recall a few others things that had happened in the last few days. Maybe they were relevant.

I had prayed to saints and talked to angels most of my life and more recently I had communicated with spirit guides, but I hadn't quite gotten to be friends with beings from other dimensions. I still had a few reservations about them.

The night the idea of inter-dimensional beings had been introduced to our personal development group, we were all together in a large room. We were told that beings often visited this place and they would be invited to come again very soon. There was no response from my logical mind that I could remember. I think it was so challenged that it just went directly into shutdown mode.

All the lights were turned out and the room was in complete darkness. Then, some strange lights began to flash. For the sceptic, it would have been easy to explain them away as a fake light show, but as the events unfolded I was becoming more convinced that something unexplainable was happening. I saw amazing patterns of light that others didn't see.

The other thing I saw, that nobody else saw, was a huge sand castle in the middle of the room. It was more like a fortified city. When the strange lights finished shining, once again the room was pitch black. There may have been a dozen other people there. Nobody was standing within three or four metres of me.

I began to feel a presence near my left ear. At first it felt quite comfortable but as it came closer I became anxious. It felt like someone was standing next to me and breathing into my ear. It was freezing cold and I heard a muffled voice and a word sounding something like, *Petunia.*

Whatever was happening, it was happening against the side of my face. It was a real sensation, a real sound, and real fear was rising. If I had been in that room on my own, I would have been terrified.

Now that I was back home, sitting in my lounge room with all that was familiar around me, I was safe enough to explore what had happened over the past few days. I believe that somehow I fell through a portal on the beach and into the great sand castle that I had seen a few days earlier.

About twelve years later, I did a past life regression. Before it began, I was asked if there were any questions I might like answers to. I thought it would be nice to know what happened on the beach that day.

This time I remembered where I went and what I saw. I was in what appeared to be a huge underground closed in cave, standing on a high elevated platform, watching what was happening far below me. I wasn't particularly interested in what they were doing. Two 'friends' were with me, assuring me that they bring no harm, and all was well. They often show up, presenting as tall silver rectangular beings with exquisite turquoise inlays.


There was a time I would have disassociated from anyone who was interested in anything psychic, paranormal or esoteric. Was it because I was keeping the rules of others, or was it because I was afraid of the unknown.

I have learnt that the unknown is my friend not my foe, waiting to introduce me to many new and exciting adventures. I also know that my mind doesn't know the difference between fear and excitement. It believes what I tell it.

How I interpret my emotions, and what I tell my mind is deeply affected by what is unresolved hiding within. Opening to the unknown needs trust, but it also asks that you identify your beliefs and dismiss those that are creating fear and holding you captive.

# The presence at the crown

## Crown Chakra

The journey to the crown can be a long and arduous pathway if you don't understand that you are surrounded with loving support at every moment and at every crossroad. You are never alone.

The somewhat overwhelming energy of the crown can let you know that someone or something far greater than yourself is present. This energy can show you that nothing is impossible, and more than often brings the unexpected.

The journey to the crown can also be a difficult road to travel if you insist on being in control. Relinquishing control asks for trust. Trust requires vulnerability, and vulnerability leaves you in a precarious position, but only when you don't believe that spirit is always with you, life is exactly the way it is meant to be, and all is well.

Time, the great illusion, can also be an enemy of the journey. It is something that measures the things of earth. You always have enough time. You never run out. You won't leave until you have finished what you came to do. Spirit is outside of time, and working in spirit time can challenge the parameters of time as we know it.

While I have countless stories of helpful intervention from angels and others that I cannot visibly see, there are other stories about presence: a presence so intense and all-powerful, that words might not express that which it emanates.

If we are God, as I believe we are, then this presence is the essence of who we are. This all-encompassing, unexplainable goodness is what the crown opens to us. Its power is such that you may tend to withdraw. The mind is intimidated as it tries to understand what it has confronted.

As a reflexology practitioner for sixteen years, I also incorporated other modalities, especially energy work. Some clients only came for energy healings, and sometimes I had the privilege of seeing things that were happening in other dimensions.

The mother of a young family was brought to see me. She was suffering with a disease, and while she was becoming more and more disabled, it was not terminal as such. She was expecting many more years to enjoy with her family. She wanted energy work.

She couldn't walk on her own, so she was helped into the chair. About the first thing she asked me was, "Will this cure me?"

I answered, "I don't know, but I do know that whatever you contracted to do in this lifetime, this treatment will help you achieve it."

Almost immediately, I became aware of a presence surrounding us. My first response was a feeling of being absolutely overwhelmed. I thought I was going to burst into tears, but I fought them back. And while I may have felt the radiance of that energy field for only a short time, the impact was unforgettable.

Why had it come? What was it doing? I didn't know, but I did know something profound changed in that moment which would help this woman achieve whatever it was that she came to do. The treatment finished and she left.

During the next session, she lay on the table. She talked about the about the disease she had, and how it had been in the family for several generations. She had been focused on not getting it.

In trying not to think about something, you can't help but think about it. So, her thoughts were focused on this hereditary disease in one way or another.

The disease targeted the muscles, and muscles are related to being pulled in two directions, and divided loyalties. She had given up something she dearly wanted to achieve, to keep others happy.

The woman only came a few times, and would rebook before she left.

The last time she came, she lay on the massage table and I was standing near her head. Her husband was sitting in the room waiting for her to finish her treatment.

All of a sudden, it was as though I was watching a video. I saw this woman rise from the table dressed in a long orange robe. Together with her husband, they went to the end of the bed and picked up a piece of paper.

They stood there having a discussion over the contents, and then proceeded to write something extra; they both signed it. I thought to myself, *this is some sort of contract they're signing. They're making an agreement.*

The treatment finished and they left.

A few weeks later, I had a phone call to say that she had died very suddenly. While it was a great tragedy for the family, I believe I saw her and her husband make an agreement for her to leave. Each gave consent. I witnessed their farewell in spirit which was nowhere near as sad and painful as the physical farewell from her family.

The crown asks us to set aside logic and the need to understand, and trust that all is as it is meant to be. Life is perfect. There are no mistakes.

I somehow know that the radiant presence who came on her first visit helped her to fulfil her contract.

There was another time when a similar presence once again revealed itself to me in such a way that I could recognise that something profound was passing through my time and space.

Before I went to the Ho'oponopono conference in Hawaii, I found myself in hospital with the face infection, which I learnt was called erysipelas. After a couple of nights in the short stay ward, I was sent to the day surgery area for a few nights.

There were four beds in the room, but only one other person. She had been there for three weeks. I didn't speak to her. A nurse told me that the woman was still there because her wound wouldn't heal. The open lesion was about 30 millimetres long, but what I didn't know, at the time, was that it would be fully healed within a few hours.

The night nurse arrived after 11 pm with my antibiotics. She was late as there were some staff issues. She was in such a hurry that she injected the antibiotic too quickly, dislodging the cannula, causing quite a mess and a stinging pain.

Eventually everything calmed down and she left.

That's when I found myself watching an imaginary story about a little pearl that lived under a crustacean: a strange shell that looked like a star fish. They lived in a cave, on the bottom of the ocean, in dark and murky waters.

The little pearl didn't know it could leave, but then, there were many things it didn't know.

It shone like a diamond, but couldn't see it.

It was different, but didn't know that being different was okay.

It was brave, but didn't feel it.

The shell that had protected it for many years helped it escape. Together they rose from the ocean's floor, noticing as they went, how those left behind were being shielded from seeing such a sight.

The little pearl had left the darkness behind, but as it floated on the ocean's surface, far from sight and view, it was still hiding.

And so, the little pearl came to be placed on display in a beautiful cabinet, in a prominent place, for all to admire. The pearl and the strange crusty shell that had protected, encouraged and helped it, sat proudly together and shone like a diamond and a star.

When we listen to Spirit, we realise that all the guidance we receive has its own unique expression, directed at our own individual needs for that particular moment and time. This was no different. Considering that I was clearing the family line of insignificance which had been expressed in many different shapes, forms and symptoms over the years, the scenario that I watched was perfect for my understanding.

I was the little pearl who had been hidden away for many years. Escaping my darkness was not enough. I had to put on display what I had learnt. And, more importantly, realise that which had kept me in darkness was also that which brought me to the light.

My father's family line held a history of conservatism, dependability, responsibility, practical caution, loyalty to old ways, and structured conforming. This needed to change.

The family line lacked confidence to shine in its own glory, with all its unique idiosyncrasies, and was unable to display flare, panache and grandeur.

This also was my battle.

Sometime I won and held the position. Sometimes I retreated, and sometimes I lost. For now, this battle was over: the war was ended; the war was won.

As I lay in my hospital bed pondering the profound wisdom that had just visited me, I felt a sense of peace within. I was taken from this third dimension to a place of oneness, a place so beautiful that I described it as *somewhere beyond tears*.

I felt a presence. Something magnificent stood before me, and to my left.

It said, "I am free."

I thought it was my father.

I said, "How do I know this is not my imagination?"

It replied, "You will know it, by the name, when the last crustacean leaves."

Crustacean was the term used to describe the shell that protected the pearl. What was the last crustacean? Was it the crust on my unhealed nose, or the shell that I hid under for many years?

And, whose name would I know? Was it my father or was it my grandmother?

I think they were both there that night, but I think the presence on the left was my grandmother, a quiet and unassuming woman who passed through life almost unnoticed.

And the name? I published my second book, *Wisdom in Retrospect* under her name: Emma Gilbert.

I was not hiding. I was putting my grandmother on display, an insignificant woman who needed to be acknowledged.

To reach my crown on this particular journey, I needed to recognise the beliefs and patterns that had kept me in darkness, accept help, and be brave enough to leave my cave. I needed to come to the surface and put myself on show. By stretching my boundaries and moving out of my comfort zone, I somehow helped to free my family line of skin problems.

There will be many journeys to my crown during my lifetime. Each one will take a different pathway, and each one will offer me opportunities to revisit that which holds me in darkness.

# Enjoy your Journey

*If the facts don't fit the theory, change the facts.*
Albert Einstein

As we continue along our journey to crown, our pathway will be strewn with concepts, ideas and theories. Some will be embraced as a homecoming, while others will be challenges and contradictions.

What is a theory to one will be a fact to another. And, what is fact to another will be only a possibility to someone else. Nothing is definite, as we discover that everything in this universe is relative to something or someone else. Every fact and every theory is relevant. Nothing is definite. Nothing is fixed.

Facts are events or things known to have happened, something proven. Theory is abstract knowledge or reasoning, something not applied or practical, a possibility. Everything that is now fact was once a theory, and every theory has the possibility to become a fact.

Our innate knowing asks that we find what is of value to each of us, and hold firm to it. Whether that is believing in a theory and searching for facts to support it, or discovering a fact and finding theories to challenge it.

One particular theory that has been proven over and over again is something Albert Einstein once said: *We cannot solve our problems with the same thinking we used when we created them.*

So in contemplating our wellness, health and lifestyle, we may need to consider what we believe and think, and change those beliefs and thoughts that are not conducive with our highest potential, optimum wellness and an abundant lifestyle.

And so, we reach the end of this particular journey together. Along the way, I hope you have learnt how to recognise the messages of your body, and also those of your lifestyle. I hope you take the time and patience to pause and put your own puzzle together, and understand what your higher consciousness is trying to draw your attention to.

172

It takes courage to look below the surface, and move outside your comfort zone. It takes trust to act on what you have learnt. As you act on what you know, wisdom gently and slowly overshadows you, and without you really understanding how, you know that you have reached a special place, where you will rest a while, before you continue on.

May your imagination open your mind to new and exciting theories.
May you hold those theories close to your heart, as you search for the facts to support them.

May you always be open to possibility and alternative paths to wellness,
May you have the courage to look deeply within to find them.

May every journey to your crown be an adventure.
As you discover that life is perfect, all is well, and everything has always been on your terms.

# Appendix

## Body systems

This general overview of the body systems is short and basic. Further information is available online or in my book, *Holistic Reflexology the eight principles.*[12]

The Nervous System gathers information from inside and outside the body (sensory/afferent input), integrates it and activates a response (motor/efferent output).
Focus: Control, communication and interpretation.
Associated with: Ignored potential, biased filters, misinterpreting, feeling delicate, unable to function as an individual, and habitual patterns of communication.

The Endocrine System consists of ductless organs that secrete regulatory substances (hormones) directly into the circulation. These hormones target specific organs in the endocrine system and allow them to produce their own hormones. It monitors through negative feedback.
Focus: Authority figures, taking direction and learning through negative feedback.
Associated with: Co-operation, sabotage, closed mind, burning yourself out, imbalance, redirection, assertiveness, expecting the worst, unable to tap into personal resources and not using resources to their best advantage.

The Cardiovascular System takes oxygen from the lungs to the tissues and carbon dioxide from the tissues to the lungs, transports nutrients and

---

[12] *Holistic Reflexology, the eight principles* published in 2010 is available as a download from www.holisticreflexology.com.au or in printed form from most online book sellers or the publisher www.feedaread.com

metabolic substances to the tissues, removes waste products to the kidneys and other excretion organs, and maintains the balance of fluid.
Focus: Flow, blockages and being on the right track.
Associated with: The good of the whole, going with the flow, cycles, sticking together, ganging up, closed ranks and the initial response.

The Lymphatic System and Immunity consists of vessels, nodes and organs without a pump to aid the cardiovascular system. It also plays an important role in body defence.
Focus: Picking up after others, self-protection, the enemy and self-criticism.
Associated with: Dumping on someone, emotional boundaries, ready for battle, expecting an attack, needing to learn something, having someone forced upon you, revenge and over-reacting.

The Skeletal System is composed of bones, joints and connective tissue. It supports posture by providing an internal framework, protects vulnerable organs, allows movement and provides storage. It gives strength, definition and shape.
Focus: Structure, restructure and infrastructure.
Associated with: Inner strength, temporary support, connecting or disconnecting from others, tearing apart, holding on, wearing thin, keeping everything in place, cushioning and flexibility.

The Muscular System maintains posture, provides movement, stabilises joints and generates heat.
Focus: Divided loyalties and being pulled in two directions.
Associated with: Carrying loads, relaxation, reaching out, habitual behaviour, time out, lifetime commitments, following the leader and automatic responses.

The Digestive System breaks down ingested food into particles small enough to be absorbed into the blood, assimilates what is beneficial and disposes of the residue.
Focus: Process, discernment and teamwork.
Associated with: Sharing a confined space, needing time to finish off, utilising resources, closing off from the past, moving forward, dead-ends, letting go, biting off more than you can chew, detoxing, regrowth and regeneration.

The Respiratory System inhales air, bringing oxygen to the blood, and exhales the carbon dioxide waste from the blood back into the air.
Focus: Give and take, fair exchange and transitions.

Associated with: Sharing, saying what others want to hear, changing direction, offering help that isn't wanted, repetitive thoughts, blocking your life force, constriction and suffocating.

The Urinary System clears the body of nitrogenous wastes, and regulates water, electrolytes and acid-base balance of the blood.
Focus: Monitoring, balance, recycling, endings and difficult decisions.
Associated with: Slow progress, impatience, holding back, storing up and release.

The Reproductive System is concerned with reproducing the offspring of a species.
Focus: To develop creative expression.
Associated with: Maturing, new beginnings, coming together, finding a safe haven, joining the real world, competition, passive aggression, swimming against the tide, being strangled, cut off, shafted and set aside, Also defines masculinity and femininity.

The Integumentary System includes the skin, the outer covering of the body, the nails and hair.
Focus: Defining boundaries, security and a willingness to be on show.
Associated with: Keeping too much out, letting too much in, your first line of defence, blocked pathways, cooling down and protecting sensitivity.

The Special Senses respond to different types of energetic stimuli.
Focus: A way to remember.
Associated with: Vision and seeing, hearing and listening, activating awareness, to sample and assess, and to heal or hurt.

## Cancer overview

Cancer is a group of diseases involving abnormal cell growth with the potential to invade or spread to other parts of the body. Cancer cells have lost their sense of identity. They don't know who they are, and where they belong. They grow and multiply in inappropriate places.

Therefore, the many forms of cancer could be a message about a person's sense of identity, as they no longer know who they are and where they belong. They may have lost their sense of self as their identity became intertwined or dependent on another. They may be confused as to the purpose, value and meaning of their life, or their identity may have been connected to what they did not who they intrinsically are.

## Autoimmune overview

An autoimmune disorder occurs when the body can't recognise the pathogen that is causing injury to the cells, subsequently attacks their own body tissues by mistake, and is then unable to correctly regulate its immune response.

On a metaphysical level, it could indicate a person who cannot accurately recognise the source of a threat, or identify the real enemy. They may be unable to recognise what belongs to them and what doesn't, and be extremely self-critical. This disorder could indicate someone who overreacts and doesn't know when enough is enough.

Autoimmunity is related to finding an appropriate response in relation to a specific issue.

Can't recognise the enemy: confusion around or inability to recognise a genuine or perceived threat.

Attacks the wrong person: the action being taken may not be directed in the right direction.

Doesn't know when to stop: unable to regulate and monitor an appropriate response.

## Infection and Inflammation

Infection is different to inflammation.

Infection is caused by harmful disease carrying agents that cause injury to the cells.

Inflammation is part of the immune response to eliminate the cause of the infection, and begin the repair process.

An infection can be caused by a virus or bacteria. Bacteria are alive, while viruses are basically non-living and dormant unless invading the cells of a host. Bacteria can be killed by antibiotics whereas viruses are more resilient.

As with any immune response, the body needs to monitor it closely. Too little inflammation may be ineffective to the healing process. Too much inflammation can compromise the cells and lead to other diseases. A response from the immune system infers that an enemy is present and has been detected. When antibodies are involved, an old and recognised enemy is present.

In either cause someone/something is invading your space/territory without invitation. Alternatively, you could be the invader, and need to pull back a little.

## Bacteria

Bacteria are single celled microbes, extremely small, often grow or live in colonies, and do not need a host to survive. They were one of the first life forms on earth, and have survived in many different environments and varieties over millions of years. Only a small percentage of bacteria are able to cause disease in people.

Harmful bacteria could be a message about:

The enemy is connected to a group or like-minded people.

Strength in numbers.

Working together to be effective.

The enemy will be here for a long time.

Strongly resisting something/someone.

## Virus

A virus needs a host to begin the process. It infiltrates the host cells and lives inside them. On a metaphysical level, a virus is ineffective without something to attach itself to.

A virus could be a message about:

Being part of a process, possibly unconsciously, that could cause harm.

An enemy who can only cause damage if they take something from you.

Defences being down which allows the enemy to enter and do damage.

Someone or something you don't want is attaching themselves to you.

Someone trying to change you and make you more like them.

## Emotions

Emotions are neither good nor bad. They are simply a way for the body to let you know that there is a situation that needs addressing. It is the memories and biases that are held in the subconscious that dictate how you name, identify or describe them.

While emotions may rise quickly and intensely, you do not need to wallow in them. Problems arise when you ignore their purpose and allow yourself to become overwhelmed and immersed in a cloud of negativity. Once you understand them as a guiding light you will become open to the messages they carry with them.

As energy and matter are interchangeable, problems can arise in the physical body when you deny, ignore, suppress or contain them. By changing form and presenting as matter, they can have a greater impact on your attention.

There are usually several contributing factors to an illness or disease. If one of these organs is under stress in any way, then it could be holding compacted emotions. The density of the suppressed emotion could prevent the organ from performing at optimal efficiency.

One aspect of the healing process could be your willingness to release the emotion that is holding this pain and discomfort in your body.

The lungs hold on to grief and guilt.
The liver hides anger and resentment.
The heart contains joy and over-stimulation.
The stomach covers up anxiety and stress.
The kidneys bury fear, terror and phobia.

## Left and right

Understanding the implications of the left and right gives further information as to who or what might be related to the cause of the problem.

Left:
Feminine, female, women.
Being, unconscious, intuition, nurturing, passive, spiritual, mother principle.
Present and future.

Right:
Masculine, male, men.
Doing, conscious, logic, supply, aggressive, physical, father principle.
Past.

A problem with the hips on the left side of the body could infer power games with a female; on the right side, power games with a male. A left hip problem could also infer problems with a creative pursuit of a male. Right hip could be related to a physical issue with money and security.

Taking into consideration the overall circumstances of a person can help to isolate the meaning of left or right for each individual.

# References and general reading

Holistic Reflexology, the eight principles, Glenda Hodge, FeedARead.com Publishing, 2014
Wisdom in Retrospect, Emma Gilbert, FeedARead.com Publishing 2014
Collins Australian Dictionary, 10th edition, HarpersCollins Glasgow, 2009
Thresholds of the Mind, Bill Harris, Centerpointe Research Institute, 2002
Essentials of Human Anatomy and Physiology Fifth Edition. Elaine N. Marieb, The Benjamin/Cummings Publishing Company, Inc. 1997
Miller-Keane Encyclopaedia & Dictionary of Medicine, Nursing and Allied Health, Sixth Edition, W B Saunders Company 1972

Online general reading and information:
https://en.wikipedia.org/wiki/
http://www.youtube.com/watch?v=OL972JihAmg
(Interviews with Dr Ihaleakala Hew Len, H'oponopono)

Lightning Source UK Ltd.
Milton Keynes UK
UKOW04f0735250717
305996UK00001B/130/P